# Oops!
## I'm The Manager!

*Getting Past "What Do I Do Now¿!"*

*in 5 Easy Steps*

Oops! I'm The Manager!
*Getting Past "What Do I Do Now¿!" in 5 Easy Steps*

Published by Giacalone and Associates LLC
First edition — August 2009
Printed in the USA

ISBN: 1-4392-4869-9
Library of Congress Control Number: 2009906720

Visit The Corporate Nanny's blog at www.thecorporatenanny.net

*To My Mom and Dad for their love, support and encouragement throughout my life.*

*And to all of the amazing managers who taught me the real ways of the world – and to the ones I look forward to meeting!*

## Acknowledgments

I would like to take this opportunity to thank my family, friends and clients for encouraging and supporting me throughout my first endeavor as an author.

To my clients – who were willing to freely offer their insights, wisdom and time.

To my friends, especially Cecilia, Charlene, Dedie and Maggie – who were there for me when I needed a push or a kick in the pants to "keep on keeping on."

To my John & Maria and Joseph & Maria – who always include me in their families' lives.

To my Nicholas, Sarah and Gianna who keep Aunt Kathy on her toes and whom I will always treasure.

To my friend and writing coach (and re-writing coach), Jon – I'll miss your "Oy" emails!

To my Robyn, Kate and Sandra for their invaluable help in making this book happen!

To my special friend and client – Annie – who originally dubbed me "The Corporate Nanny™" – for all of her time and confidence in me and my work.

To my Larry – who is always patient and loving and was supportive when I needed him – whether he was feeding his cells in his lab – or hanging drywall in the house.

To everyone – I will always be thankful!

# Contents

CHAPTER ONE

# Oops!

During a mid-morning recess back in elementary school, I remember drawing a hopscotch grid in chalk on the asphalt schoolyard. While I was writing the numbers, Mrs. Ostensow called Freddy Fabrini and me over. Obediently, we stopped what we were doing and came to her side.

"I want you two to pick teams for a game of dodge ball," she informed us. Freddy and I were not overly athletic – in fact, we were both on the nerdy side of the "cool" scale. We looked at each other and I saw a glimmer of fear in his eyes – the same fear I was suddenly overcome with too. In that instant, I was thrown into my first management situation. "Oops! I'm the manager!"

It happens all the time. We fall into opportunities instead of finding our way there through hard work and planning. Whether it's finding the love of your life as you search for your dropped keys in the grocery store parking lot, discovering an incredible pair of shoes as you stand in line at the Post Office or grabbing a major promotion because you were the first person to show up at a staff meeting, the world really does revolve around the axis of chance and happenstance. Being in the right place at the right time is usually a blessing – but also has its perils.

## Stumbling Up the Corporate Ladder

You won't believe how often managers tell me they don't know how they got their job. There was no formal announcement or interview process – all of a sudden, they were managers. In fact, that's what happened to me. It seemed like one day I was a worker bee and the next day I was the manager. I didn't ask for the position, but I found myself in a new role anyway.

I like to call this "stumbling up the corporate ladder." Yes, most of us work very hard and we like to think that we will be promoted to the next level because of our competence, wisdom or skill. But the truth is, climbing the ladder of success is often really stumbling our way up, and not by strategic planning on our part. Stumbling up is not a bad thing – it still represents success through hard work. If you weren't working hard to begin with, you probably wouldn't be at the company you're with. The stumbling is fine – it's how you stand up and dust yourself off that really matters.

My youngest brother remembers a domestic violence call he received on his first day as a sergeant – the first supervisory level in the Police Department. He called his squad together, hopped into the car and started to drive. When they arrived on the block, he asked, "Who has the street number?" His squad looked around at each other – no one had the information. One of the officers said, "Sarge – what do we do now?" Frustrated, my brother replied, "Whadaya asking me for – I was you yesterday!" As he was about to ream out his squad, a TV came flying through a window – they had stumbled onto the right house.

Now, not everyone stumbles into a management job – some go through the traditional interview process to be hired. But many of these intentional managers were not aware of what they were signing up for – yes, more money and getting off the shop floor might have been great reasons to apply. But if you're in this spot, you probably didn't know the harsh reality of what would be expected in the job. Not to worry – this book is for you, too.

## The Repercussions

Sadly, many companies promote staff to management positions without adequate training. And even in organizations that do try to offer management training (bless their hearts), they focus on theory rather than practical application. So, as you stumble up the ladder, you keep your balance until you can make your next stumble up. That's why you – and zillions of other managers – are scouring the shelves for management advice, and why you're reading this book. I hear you, "Help! Give me a clue!"

That's what this book will do. In fact, it will give you more than clues – it will give you the knowledge you need to be a happy and productive manager. These are strategies I've learned through my own years of stumbling up the management ladder and the experiences I've had helping my clients.

## Walking in Your Shoes

Believe me, I've been exactly where you are – a frustrated manager wondering what to do.

Early in my management career, my boss – a friend then and even more so today — followed me into the Ladies' Room and furiously harpooned me about my management style. It seemed I had a reputation for quickly shooting down other people's ideas, and everyone on the team was frustrated with me. I distinctly remember her words, "A steamroller couldn't give you feedback!" Who knew? Everyone but me, apparently! The signs were there – I just wasn't seeing them.

So my boss hired a management consultant to facilitate our meetings and figure out why we weren't communicating well. Now, you might think I would be highly offended at an outsider being brought in, but no, I was all for it. Once I got over the sting of the "steamroller" comment, I was eager to make things work. Well, 30 minutes into our first meeting, the consultant stopped the meeting and asked me to step outside. The feedback she gave me changed my work life forever.

"You see things before anyone else sees them, so you're quick to say no to ideas that you know won't work," she said. "But you frustrate people when you constantly shoot down their ideas. Try letting the ideas float instead. Be curious, ask questions and engage in a dialogue rather than 'machine gunning' questions at them."

Huh? Was that really how I was perceived? And what's wrong with being a straight shooter, laying it on the line and calling it as I see it anyway? But, figuring I didn't have much to lose at this point, I tried it her way and guess what? It worked! It was painful for me to change the way I interacted. But when I did, and got positive results for my efforts, things got 100 percent better for me and for the team. It was the best piece of advice I never asked for!

## The Corporate Nanny

In the spring of 2008, I was flying to Scottsdale for a two-day senior management meeting and, of course, the plane was late. Everyone was waiting for me in the lobby to board the "corporate limo" – a 15-passenger bus – to take us to a dinner that would kick off the first part of the meeting. I hate being late, and on top of that knowing I was keeping everyone waiting, I was feeling a bit harried (to say the least!). When I entered the lobby, my friend and client – the president of a successful business – greeted me with, "Look everyone – here's our Corporate Nanny!" We boarded the bus and began our journey.

I was in such a rush and worried that everyone was starving

(my Italian heritage peeking through) that the greeting didn't really hit me until hours later. Maybe I am The Corporate Nanny! After all, I built my business on helping organizations become more effective with regard to the people side of their business; pointing out things that my clients didn't want to face, but knew they had to fix – all with compassion and humor, of course.

## Which is Why You're Reading On

So, after your initial shock of "Oh my! What do I do now?!" wears off, your second realization begins – how do I do it?!

The good news is that you already know what to do – but probably haven't really thought about it from a common sense perspective. Over the years, you've learned the skills you need – from the playground to the workplace. What separates comfortable managers from the overwhelmed is the ability to step back, recognize the issue, look around for clues, start working on solving the situation and remembering "The Forgotten Five."

# CHAPTER TWO

# The Neglected Knowledge

**(aka The Forgotten Five©)**

When I was hired as a VP of Human Resources at a start-up biotech company, to be honest – I was completely overwhelmed. The highest position I'd held up to that point was as a director of another large company, where I managed my own division and had never really been involved in other facets of the HR Department. Suddenly, I was in charge of everything from the ground up: recruiting and hiring for more than 600 jobs in a sleepy East Coast town, and hiring my own staff to make this happen – all in about 90 days! I could have collapsed under the pressure – and trust me, there were many times I wanted to give up and run away. I had a supportive boss, but not a patient one.

I know that I was hired for my common sense. There were other applicants who had more experience, but the CEO believed I had the innate ability to tell it like it is. So, I called on the skills I had developed over the years – the same principles I am giving to you – and put them to work using common sense. The initial hiring plan was completed on time with great success. Since then, the company has gone in new directions, but the policies my staff and I created are still in place and are guiding it forward.

Now, as every Nanny knows, it's important to give instructions clearly and in a language appropriate to the situation. I don't want to bore or scare you with office-speak such as "principle," or "analyze" or heaven forbid, "strategy" – but that is what this lesson calls for, so let's work through this.

## The Neglected Knowledge: The Forgotten Five

So what are these lessons? They are simple, really – determining the personalities involved, using respect and humor to address the situation, exposing and facing the truth and putting it all together.

I told you – these are simple principles that you already know. But, like most first-time managers, directors or executives, in the heat of the moment, we forget to use them – all of them. Missing just one of these skills could lead to more stress and rocky roads. Management is like baking – both are tinkering with chemistry. When you're baking cookies, you've got to use all of the ingredients – flour, salt, butter, sugar and a rising agent. You might be tempted to leave out an ingredient to make the cookies "healthier," but, you'll end up with a mess in the kitchen – and awful cookies!

The same goes for the workplace – skip one of these principles and the situation will never be fully resolved without a mess.

These five principles are introduced below and explained in further detail in subsequent chapters. They are not formal rules or scientifically proven theories, but practical knowledge I have learned and sharpened through my experiences with companies and social situations over the years. You already know this information – you've just most likely forgotten to use it. Hence the name "The Neglected Knowledge: The Forgotten Five." I'm just here to remind you of them.

## Playground Personalities

Wouldn't it be nice to have a special label on our foreheads so others know exactly what type of person we are? Well, I haven't been able to figure out how to do that yet, but I do know that if you listen to and observe folks carefully, you can begin to figure out just what makes people tick.

Knowing the players lets you size up a situation with greater skill – including where you fit in! There are as many personalities as there are people in the workforce. But when pared down to the core, I can think of four main Playground Personalities: the Peacemaker, the Organizer, the Revolutionary and the Steamroller. You met these people years ago when you were a kid on the playground, and the personalities hold true for any playground where you currently find yourself. Most people are a composite of psyches, but still predominantly one style over another. Using all of them is the trick. Knowing who is who can make the here and now a lot easier for everyone.

If you're a **Peacemaker**, you appreciate communication and collaboration. You care about others and want to be sure everyone is happy. You're loyal and have high integrity. Establishing relationships and building trust are very important to you. Okay, so you could stand to be more thick-skinned. But your need for encouragement and recognition transfers to the encouragement you give to your team. So what if the mere sound of the word "conflict" sends you running for coffee or chocolate to soothe your nerves. Your motto, "Take turns and give everyone a chance," says it all.

The **Organizer** is highly structured and decisive. If you're an Organizer, you love schedules, timelines, systems and traditions. Maybe it's true that your need for structure and systems makes you nitpick and see the negative side of things a bit too much at first – but hey, it's also what makes you so reliable and dependable. Of course, you expect your employees to act the same. Years ago you could have been seen organizing the games at recess: "Everyone line up and count off by twos...."

On the other hand, the **Revolutionary** hates routines and

schedules and prefers to adapt to the moment at hand. If you're a Revolutionary, you'd rather take your chances with a flexible atmosphere than let policies and procedures get in the way. You may, at times, be criticized for kicking in the door first and asking questions later. And some of your bosses might frown upon what they see as your anti-establishment attitude. But your outgoing, action-oriented style makes you fun to be with. "I know the rules say that, but let's play it this way instead today..." was your mantra way back when and, when translated into your work style, there's never a dull moment on your team.

Last, but not forgotten (as s/he will let you know), is the **Steamroller**. If you're a Steamroller at heart (like me), you might have been known as the playground Bully. Not the one who steals the little kids' lunch money and knocks them down – but the know-it-all with thousands of ideas to impart to others. Your enthusiasm could be mistaken for arrogance, and many times what you believe to be facts are really your opinions. And though your motto was and still is, "If you would just listen to what I'm saying you'd see it my way," above all, you value competency in others.

I can hear you think, "Okay, Nanny – why did you address the personalities to me directly? Isn't the point of this to help me analyze my staff?"

Yes, this is a great way to figure out how to work with your staff, but the truth is, if you don't know who you are, you can never manage anyone effectively. It's like the old adage, "You can't love another if you don't love yourself."

Before you can change the way you manage people, you have to recognize your personality. Sure, it may be painful at first, just as it was hard for me to see that I was steamrolling my team's ideas. Am I a Steamroller in every sense? No. I can identify with many traits of the Organizer, the Revolutionary, and even the

Peacemaker – after all, who doesn't want harmony in the office?

Whatever you are thinking, don't panic! I know this is a lot to get into. So, we'll save the details for the next chapter.

## Facing Facts

In my role as a consultant, I am blessed with the virtue of distance, and not having any political "skin in the game." As an outsider looking in, I can often see the heart of the matter clearly. But as a manager, you're not always able to see the forest through the trees – or maybe you do and just don't want to deal with the situation, hoping it may correct itself. The situation/issue/ sticking point that has your team all tied up is probably as clear as day – but because you have to deal with conflict, hurt feelings or worse yet having to address the staff, the issue is ignored and the rug gets higher and higher from the dust and dirt swept underneath!

Discovering the truth – and facing up to it – is probably the hardest part of management. No one likes to determine blame or come face-to-face with harsh realities that might affect their friends and staff. But ignoring this vital strategy will make you an unhappy, ineffective and unpopular manager.

## R-E-S-P-E-C-T

In the heat of the moment, it's easy to blurt out the first thought that comes to mind. Usually this shot from the hip is an unintended insult. Most people don't even realize they're doing it.

Blaming your reaction on a quick, knee-jerk response won't cut it, especially as a manager. But learning how to control your reactions isn't the way to overcome this hurdle either. Learning to treat each other with respect is the best way to go.

The Queen of Soul might pronounce, "R-E-S-P-E-C-T, find out what it means to me," but in the workplace, it's about finding out what it means for one and all.

Treating others appropriately and choosing your words to suit their individual styles helps keep all the personalities in check. Doing so will lead to a workplace full of peace and harmony (most of the time anyway!). Failing to do so, unfortunately, can lead to costly problems that will fester for years.

I honestly believe you can catch more flies with honey than vinegar. So let's buzz around this idea and see how you can create the sweet taste of success.

## Funny "Hmmm," Not Funny "Ha-Ha!"

Like rehearsal on a Broadway stage, you have almost everything in order. You figured out who the players are in the scenario, you uncovered the underlying truth and you've found a way to meet everyone's style. Now is the time to step back and see the humor of the situation.

Yes, the humor. The problem might be painful and unpleasant, but there is always a factor of absurdity that makes the situation somewhat comical.

I have to stress – I am not talking about poking fun at individual people, but of the situation as a whole. On a TV comedy, while some of the characters are funny, the real humor lies in the predicament. That is why it's called a situational-comedy. Yes, the personalities all contribute to the actions, but the actions of the event are inherently funny.

Seeing the humor lets you clarify the circumstances, and this clarity will help with the final principle.

## Making It Happen!

The last principle is really about, well, tact – putting it all together to tackle the problems and reform the players with finesse. Like all of the principles, you know this one intuitively – like sensing when it's time to top off the gas tank just before the needle falls below "E" – you know when it's time to take action. You know how to speak, you've thought about what you're going to say and how to say it, now it's time to do it in an assertive, but approachable way. There's a fine line between waiting for the right time, jumping the gun or – heaven forbid – doing nothing! There are plusses and minuses for each of these, as you will come to read.

This is the communication piece of the puzzle, and for many, it's the most difficult to put into action. Do not fear – The Corporate Nanny is here to guide you through. And soon, you will be the master of the playground.

## Ready?

I never met a happy person who was a miserable manager. The baggage you carry from office to home (and back) is heavy and weighs in on every aspect of your day. That is why The Neglected Knowledge has to become second nature.

So, are you ready to dig in and get started? Yesterday you were a member of the team, and today, you're leading that team to its goals. I know it's a big switch, but as you just read, the practical knowledge to be a manager is already in you – now it's time to reshape what you knew, but forgot, into knowledge you remember and will use naturally.

I know you can do this. If *I* could, then anyone can.

# CHAPTER THREE

# The Playground Personalities

## Who is The Corporate Nanny?

From the story in the first chapter, it is clear that I am – and always will be – a Steamroller. Although this is my primary Playground Personality, it's tempered by strong "Organizer" tendencies. I rely on my intellect to think through issues and keep a tight schedule, because otherwise I may over-commit. I have to simplify my plans and actions to get everything accomplished. Yes, at times, I am also a Peacemaker and a Revolutionary, but chances are, I pull these out when I am dealing with a specific situation – a skill you'll learn about as you read on.

When I first thought about writing this book, I told my boyfriend of many years, Larry, that I was going to focus on the idea that self-awareness leads to transformation. He is always supportive – but for some reason – this concept hit him the wrong way. He laughed so hard, he almost fell out of his chair. "Do you really believe that?" he questioned. Before I could answer, he kept on going....

"You don't think you can change people, do you? I don't think people can change!" He went on to espouse his theory that self-awareness leads to self-denial or self-justification. Although I do not doubt his comment is believed by many – I truly believe that without knowing who you really are – what makes you tick – what pushes your buttons – what inspires you – what makes you happy – you will go through your work life always wondering "why" something didn't work out for you.

After collecting my thoughts, I finally said, "I know *I* can't change people – but I do believe people can change." You will figure out what Playground Personality type my boyfriend is later on, but for now you'll have to get to know yourself – which may or may not be easy!

## Who are You?

Remember I said you have to know yourself before you can manage others? Well hang on! I've never met a happy, self-confident, good communicator who turned out to suck as a manager. Yes, that was blunt – The Corporate Nanny tells it like it is. To me, an individual's state of mind and presence all contribute to his/her Playground Personality. Yes, I know we all have trials and tribulations in our lives that make living – let alone managing – difficult at times. But if you want to be happy in your manager role, help your department meet its goals, coach your staff so they are motivated, happy and productive, then you have to know yourself – cold! Yes, that includes every perception, behavior, attitude and trait.

If this sounds like a lot of hocus-pocus, then you are probably denying who you are or taking my boyfriend's point of view about change – and neither one will help you become the manager you can be.

## "I could have told you that!"

I subscribe to the theory that you have one personality that always rises to the occasion. Some people are who they are every minute of every day. If you make lists at work, there's a good chance that you are a list-maker at home. If you wake up on a Wednesday with plans for the workday, there's a good chance that when you wake up on Saturday your day is already planned.

Some say they have a work personality and real-world personality. But many folks, whether they have a separate personality for work or not, share this characteristic: **They have little idea of how others perceive them or the affect their actions, words and personalities have on those who work with them, above them and for them.**

Are they out of touch? Perhaps. What one person perceives as firm leadership, another might view as tyrannical behavior. A manager who tries to make everyone happy at the expense of effective working solutions might be observed as weak.

Throughout your work career, you have probably taken various management assessments. When the results come back, many managers are surprised and even skeptical when they identify their management style. This always surprises me because it's usually through "self-assessments" that people fall into certain categories, so unless the "self" is someone else, you need to own the results of your assessments! Yet, they report that when they share the information with their friends and families, the reaction they get is almost unanimously, "I could have told you that!" So why didn't they? If they had, you probably wouldn't have been ready to handle it, or would have dismissed the feedback. Just as it's hard for you to recognize your style, it's hard for people close to you to give you this type of feedback – especially if it's less than positive.

Chances are, this management style has been with you all your life – and like me – probably became evident on the schoolyard at recess. Bullies, organizers, leaders, followers, loners, social butterflies – these traits have been with you a long time. For many, facing the reality of who you are head-on is difficult and stressful. As frightening as the task may seem, analyzing this information is critical to figuring out how you play with others today in the workplace.

Recognizing your management style requires you to take a good look at yourself – a good, honest look.

## Why Playground Personalities?

Sitting in large, glass conference rooms overlooking amazing city skylines, listening to endless accusations of "he said this," and "she did that," I am reminded of my days in elementary school. Just as I am doing now, I was the kid who was called on to facilitate the other kids on the playground. My friends, and even teachers, would ask for my help – whether it was taking something to the principal's office, talking to one of the "trouble-makers" or consoling a friend who was upset over a poor grade. Of course, I was too young to know "why" I was being asked, but as I entered the workforce, the same phenomenon repeated itself. My bosses would give me the difficult assignments – going to business units when the staff was out of control, counseling executives who were always upset with their staff or working with managers who stayed in their office and didn't interact with their staff. I was the "fixer."

One day I was so annoyed that I was only assigned these difficult confrontations, I marched into my boss' office and demanded to know why. His response: "Kathy, you are good at sorting out the issues, getting folks to see the problems through humor and putting plans in place to make things better." "Wow," I thought, "that was great feedback." Guess I would have never known if I hadn't asked!

Managers always reminded me of being back on the playground. We are older, but essentially the same: ones who wanted to take care of something; ones who needed to be consoled; ones who needed to be reigned in; and the ones who always knew what to do.

Your personality is determined when you are very young. My friend recently unearthed his first grade report card. The teacher's comments could have been penned by his current clients. The kid who is creative and can't sit still grew into the man who manages a successful film studio and flits around the globe!

## Your Playground Personality

In the previous chapter, I touched on the four Playground Personalities: the Peacemaker, the Organizer, the Revolutionary and the Steamroller. Now it's time to delve deeper into each one and question yourself and your place in the workspace.

As you read, I urge you to think about how you may or may not fit each personality. Yes, another self-assessment! Unlike expensive, scientific batteries of tests, this one is rather informal. For it to be effective, don't respond as the way you want to be or think you are – respond as the way you are!

There are 12 questions to ask yourself for each of the Playground Personalities. Be honest and think about each answer – check the box if this describes you more than 50 percent of the time. At the end, tally your check marks. If the score is greater than 10, this is your primary Playground Personality. If you scored greater than 6 but less than 10, this is your secondary style.

Very few people are only one Playground Personality – each of us is a complex mixture of many psyches. It is very likely that you have a primary and one or two secondary styles. It's all good – and through the rest of the book, you will learn how to use your personality mix to work best with your staff.

# The Peacemaker

Remember the kid on the playground who wanted to break up the fights or get the teacher involved if s/he knew there was going to be a brawl? They were the Peacemakers!

Most of the Peacemakers I know just want to be happy at work and want others to get along. They'll go out of their way to make sure people have the appropriate equipment and resources to get their work done, often sacrificing their own needs for the sake of others. They want to do the right thing and resolve to do so at the risk of hurting feelings or alienating a member from the team. They'll bend over backwards to be advocates for their staff, even though they might not get reciprocal treatment. And for many Peacemakers, it's difficult to understand when people just don't get along.

Now, you won't find Peacemakers crying at their desks or unable to make difficult decisions – they are stronger than you think. But you'll find them making these decisions while wrapped in the corporate flags of loyalty, integrity and trust – all of which are very important to them and to how people relate to the organization.

A few years ago, a friend of mine was in a career transition and decided to start her own consulting firm. She was hugely successful – she had plenty of business and her clients loved her. Yet, she was not happy. At the gym, I asked her why? She hesitated to answer, but finally came clean – she missed having a staff, working collaboratively with others in an organization and missed going to the holiday parties. My first reaction was "Yikes! If I never have to go to another holiday party it will be too soon!" She was amused, but not placated. We talked more, lifted a few barbells and concluded that working alone was not the solution to her career transition after all. She took a top job at a cutting edge company and has been doing great ever since!

Peacemakers want to complete tasks with as little conflict as possible. They want the team to get along – for themselves to "fit in" and to genuinely care about others. When they take a stand on an issue, they can either be powerfully quiet or "in your face." Peacemakers validate a solid management relationship by being committed to their organization, staff and personal success, and believe both the organization and staff are equally committed. They may not know if someone is complaining about them, and depend on others to inform them. And when confronted with this information, they often won't admit that there may be a disconnect between them and others – after all, who wouldn't get along with a Peacemaker?

***The upside of the Peacemaker:*** When the chips are down and people are feeling uncertain, the Peacemaker is there to make sure everything is going as well as could be expected and people are feeling okay. Their need for communication usually smoothes over rough spots. Building relationships and providing rewards and recognition help put the universe back in balance!

***The downside of the Peacemaker:*** Making everyone happy at the expense of their own comfort is not good for them or the team as a whole. The personal stress of keeping the peace may be hard on their physical and emotional well-being. Their constant need to be sure everyone is happy may be perceived by others as a weakness. The need for open communications may be intimidating to some, and the dedicated loyalty to the company may be seen as "brown nosing."

## Are you a Peacemaker?

- ☐ I need to make sure everyone is okay.
- ☐ I appreciate communication.
- ☐ I am supportive of and care about others.
- ☐ I often need to identify with groups and organizations.
- ☐ I collaborate with everyone.
- ☐ I need to establish a personal connection to work with others.
- ☐ I need to build trust.
- ☐ I am loyal to the company and my staff.
- ☐ I have a high level of integrity.
- ☐ I do not like conflict.
- ☐ I am not thick-skinned.
- ☐ I need encouragement and recognition.

_____ **Total number of checks**

I once had the opportunity to work with a senior manager at a large restaurant chain in New Jersey. It just so happens that two departments in the company were trying to build a store in mid-town Manhattan, and there was a great deal of miscommunication between them. My client is organized and highly structured – her son's homework was done every night before they had dinner – and I mean every night! She couldn't understand what the issues were; couldn't they just build the restaurant? She met with the two department heads individually to understand where they were coming from. One department had secured the bid for development and the other department was having trouble fulfilling the bid within the budget. She asked if they could work it out between themselves, using the logic that "We're all part of one company so couldn't everyone just get along?" When both department heads came back to her with a resounding "no," she called for The Corporate Nanny. She asked for my help, and I accepted. After a lengthy consultation, her parting words to me were, "At the end of the day, I just want everyone to get along!" My first thought was – "Oh my, that restaurant is never going to be built!"

A Peacemaker working with two different Playground Personalities – were they doomed from the start? Not necessarily so. Knowing who you are and the Playground Personalities of those you work with can help you create successful strategies to cope with almost every situation. I will tell you the restaurant did get built and is thriving!

# The Organizer

How far back can you remember your first organizing thought? Or better yet – did you ever have one? When I was about eight, my mother, an Organizer/Peacemaker, spent a great deal of time writing a "To Do" list of chores on a chart for me, which she hung inside my clothes closet. It was a detailed list, and the chart was pretty large. I was rewarded with a gold star whenever I completed a task. Every day when I woke up, I went to the list to see what I could accomplish before I left for school – there were usually one or two things I could do. When I came home from school, I would run back to the list – and sure enough, the stars were there! Obviously, I was completely motivated by the stars!

When my middle brother turned eight, my mother dutifully put together a chart of chores for him and hung it inside his closet. When he came home from school and went to hang up his coat, he freaked out when he saw the list! He ripped it off the closet door and raced into the kitchen. My poor mother stood horrified – she couldn't have imagined what made him so upset. "Mom," he said, "I don't need a list, and I won't use one – so if you want me to do something just ask!" She looked at me with a confused expression – she couldn't understand how her two children could react so differently to the same parenting method.

Lists are just an example of how Organizers lead their lives. Whether they keep their To-Do lists in a PDA or on Post-it Notes, lists are something near and dear to an Organizer's heart – and the key tool Organizers use.

Organizers are highly structured. They plan timelines and need to know which responsibilities are assigned to whom. They anticipate pitfalls, and they always have a backup plan ready for action! Their mantra is usually "everything has a place." Organizers have regularly scheduled maintenance plans worked out for their cars, computers and heating systems, spring and fall cleanings – even garbage can cleaning. At work, the Organizer will make the time to clean out files, desk drawers, miscellaneous papers and bookcases. It makes them feel good!

For me, Organizing is my happy place – especially when I'm under a lot of stress. People think of managing as it relates to work, but in reality, we manage more at home than we do in the office – and the skills you've developed are used in both places.

When my father was diagnosed with a heart valve blockage and needed a triple by-pass, my family was thrown into chaos. I received a phone call from each of my brothers – each pleading "We don't know what you need us to do, but we'll do whatever you say." Let's see – meeting the doctor, scheduling the surgery, buying three-months' worth of household goods so my mother didn't have to run to the store every day – my Organizer list was already forming in my head!

So, I sat down and formalized the list, using my favorite

"bucket technique" (making random lists and categorizing them). I labeled the buckets "Pre-Op," "While At Hospital" and "Post-Op." Three buckets and three siblings – this was a snap! I assigned John the Pre-Op activities; after all, he is a trained investigator, so he would be able to interview the doctors. I assigned Joseph the "At Hospital" list, as he was calm in emergency situations, never needed a lot of sleep and was never afraid to challenge the status-quo anywhere, even at a hospital. That left me the Post-Op activities, since I may be more nurturing than the guys. The result: everything worked out well. The organization allowed for open communications – which you need in a time of crisis. There were no conflicts, no arguments and no stress. The family worked together as one – from diagnosis to full recovery.

***The upside of the Organizer:*** When things seem chaotic or out of control, the Organizer can usually sort through the issues and clearly define them. Organizers are able to create lists and action plans, make assignments and hold people accountable for the work. They are good at communicating, and know that communication is essential in times of chaos. They are not intimidating, but steadfast and approachable by others, so two-way dialogue is comfortable and effective.

***The downside of the Organizer:*** Organizers can make so many lists and timelines, they might get lost in the moment! Organizers carry their stress either internally, because they think people might not be moving fast enough and don't articulate or carry it externally, verbally (sometimes loudly) making people aware of their discontent. Working without the plan that was agreed to drives the Organizer nuts, and when they aren't multi-tasking they feel inefficient. Sometimes, Organizers can become so task-oriented that they aren't much fun to be around.

## Are you an Organizer?

- ☐ I like to manage by scheduling.
- ☐ I like details.
- ☐ I create and use timelines.
- ☐ I must close out all tasks/issues when they are completed.
- ☐ I subscribe to the "give and take" method of management.
- ☐ I live in a highly structured world.
- ☐ I am loyal to the company.
- ☐ I have a strong sense of tradition.
- ☐ I am very decisive.
- ☐ I am extremely reliable and dependable.
- ☐ On occasion, I nitpick the issues.
- ☐ On occasion, my first reaction to an issue is negative.

**_____ Total number of checks**

# The Revolutionary

At some point, both of my brothers attended the same elementary school. One day, the principal approached my mother on the playground and asked, "Do you know what the difference is between your two boys?" Fearing the worst, my mother braced herself for the response. "If there was a fight on the playground, John would try and break it up, and Joseph would be on the sidelines taking bets!" Therein lies the essence of the Revolutionary!

Revolutionaries like to work in a loose environment, where they can think, create, get things done and have fun doing it! They like a lot of action – the thought of routine work kills their spirit. You might find them playing practical jokes on others or having nicknames for people at work (usually terms of endearment). They often take risks, although sometimes without all the facts. To which they exclaim, "Who needs all the facts – we'll figure it out when we get there!" Revolutionaries are usually called into organizations during times of restructuring or turnaround events. They're great at thinking about things differently – you'll never hear a Revolutionary say, "We've always done it this way." They're fun to be around if you can hang on for the wild ride.

I remember as a young manager, there was great turmoil surrounding a project I found difficult to tackle. My staff was running in multiple directions; my timelines and lists told me one thing, but my staff and instincts told me another; and I was afraid to steer us to another course without approval. When I finally went to my boss for help, I told her of the nuttiness that was going on with the project and admitted that I didn't know what do to next.

"Do something!" she shouted. Not one of her finer moments – a fact she would attest to a few years later. I realized that sitting at my desk and making more charts or timelines was not the answer. Someone had to spring into action, so my inner-Revolutionary kicked in. I reassembled my team, brainstormed for input on the tasks we did well – and those not so well, retooled some of the non-working items and went back to the project with a different attitude. Lo and behold – it worked!

***The upside of the Revolutionary:*** They are able to brainstorm endless possibilities without getting bogged down by the "devil in the details" mentality. Revolutionaries think freely, react immediately, aren't afraid to re-do work or try something completely different – all while having fun doing so! They're calm under pressure and don't get rattled easily. They're great at multi-tasking and don't feel the need to get everything done that's on the list – if they could find the list!

*The downside of the Revolutionary:* Their need for action can have the opposite effect on their staff. The staff may shut down from the confusion over how something needs to get done – or even more basic – what needs to get done! The Revolutionary's mantra in most situations is, "Let's do it!" This can lead to miscommunication among co-workers, which in turn leads to a lot of rework. Sometimes they don't make good listeners, because they're so consumed with the plans they're implementing. Revolutionaries also can forget what they asked to have done, so follow-up can be overlooked. They're famous for saying, "You don't expect me to remember what I said, do you? I thought it was done!"

### Are you a Revolutionary?

- ☐ I am seen and heard.
- ☐ I am prone to act now and beg for forgiveness later.
- ☐ I tend to be more scattered than organized.
- ☐ I am action-oriented.
- ☐ I hate routine.
- ☐ I am fun to be with.
- ☐ I do not like policies and procedures – they tend to get in the way.
- ☐ I can clearly define structure; I just don't want to follow it.
- ☐ I am easy to get along with.
- ☐ I can be very flexible, impulsive and adaptable.
- ☐ I like to be in the moment.
- ☐ I am not reserved; instead, I am rather outgoing.
- _____ **Total number of checks**

# The Steamroller

An old friend of mine, Marsha, reminded me of a story when we were in the fifth grade together. Mr. Zapparelli, the science teacher, asked us to build a car using a sneaker – a car that would actually work! The winner would get an "all expense paid trip" to the local pizza shop during the school day. We both loved pizza and desperately wanted to win.

Well, Marsha and I were put into separate groups. My group worked well together – although I had no clue where to start, my teammates did. Our project came out okay and showed the talents of (or lack of) each member. (I was happy to hastily paint the shoe, as I am not technical).

On the other side of the room, Marsha quickly summed up her group as "so lame," that she took control. Marsha understood the "big picture," and knew what was needed to wire the circuits and to design a more efficient drive system – and to win! So, she single-handedly put together a blueprint and then assigned responsibilities. When her teammates failed her, Marsha picked up the slack and made it work – at the expense of many hard feelings! Meet a Steamroller!

The Steamrollers I know today in business share many of these same traits. They are smart, highly opinionated, can solve complex problems and are great visionaries – and they're restless. They don't "suffer fools gladly" and like to surround themselves with smart, competent people. Steamrollers constantly need to be intellectually stimulated, as they get bored very easily. Their minds are always "on" – they don't have an "off" switch. If you observe them carefully, you can see the wheels turning in their heads! Steamrollers are extremely goal-oriented and always have the end in mind. They are usually laser-beam focused – so much so they think they're done even though they might not be.

A classic Steamroller example: I was in a tense moment at a meeting when one of my clients stood up and said, "Look, this can't be that hard. We aren't engineering rocket ships here!" Translated for the rest of us – "I'm done with the brainstorming, pick one thing and do it! The sky isn't going to fall in if we have to change our plans."

Steamrollers get to the point right away, usually without taking other people's feelings into consideration. They know who they can influence, and don't waste time with those they can't influence. When people get in their way, Steamrollers will tell them what to do – and if they can't, they tell them to get out of the way!

Steamrollers have opinions about everything – even when the circumstances do not call for one. They lead their lives by opinions – especially if they don't like the facts. They live in their own reality, which may be quite different from true reality.

I remember working on a team where one person was asked to take notes from the meeting. The note taker wasn't writing too much during the meeting (as an Organizer, I would have been writing like a maniac). He transcribed his sparse notes that night and emailed them to me the next morning. When I read the email, I thought, "Boy, was I at this meeting?" Later that day, I approached the note taker and asked him what happened with the notes. He informed me, "Well, I didn't think the team was going in the right direction, so I put my own spin on the notes!" I was speechless – which takes a lot!

Although Steamrollers might ask for your opinion, the truth is – they don't really want it. They ask to gain clarity in their own minds about how they want something to be addressed. If they really want to do something, they have no need or concern about anyone else's opinions. If you get hooked into telling

Steamrollers your opinion, don't be surprised at the response! If they don't agree with you, they'll tell you you're wrong. Funny, because the last I heard, opinions can't be wrong. But this strong headedness is at the core of a Steamroller's personality – so go with it, or get out of the way!

Steamrollers like to be in charge, but have little patience when people don't rise to the occasion and shine. Sometimes, you're lucky enough to work with a Steamroller who'll tell you what you did wrong, but more often than not, you'll be kept in the dark and wonder what happened! Some clues that you fell out of grace with a Steamroller: you're dropped from emails, you're not invited to meetings, your calls go unanswered – basically all interactions stop. If you have the courage to confront a Steamroller and ask what went wrong, s/he will answer only so you can fix the problem and continue to be productive.

Lastly, one of the worst buttons you can press on a Steamroller is to say, "No, you can't do that" or "You'll never be able to do that." S/he will die trying to prove you wrong – and drive everyone nuts doing so.

I had a situation where a senior manager was flown in from a remote office and was waiting in the lobby to meet with the CEO. I saw Sam in the lobby when I arrived, but I didn't think anything of it. By the time I turned the corner to my desk, my phone rang – it was the CEO – a classic Steamroller. (In fact, he could write his own best seller on the subject). He was going to fire Sam, and wanted me in the office when he did the deed. Now, I knew that firing Sam was not the right thing to do, but I also knew I couldn't tell the CEO that he "couldn't fire Sam." In the 40-second walk from my office to his, I had to devise a plan to stop the firing.

"Look, you're the CEO, so you can do whatever you want." I took a deep breath. "I just have a few questions. Does Sam know you have issues with his work? Have you visited Sam's facility and given him feedback about what's bugging you?"

Of course the answers were "no." The room fell silent for about 30 seconds – which seemed like an eternity – then the CEO finally exhaled. "Well, maybe we shouldn't fire Sam, after all. Just write him up!" Whew! That was a close one!

***The upside of the Steamroller:*** Now I didn't mean to scare anyone. Steamrollers, for all their brashness and arrogance, also are quite brilliant and caring. They cannot acquire enough knowledge, and get charged-up by solving new projects! Interestingly enough, they fiercely protect the people they work with. Steamrollers will defend their staff to others outside the department, and when they meet with the staff member alone – they tell them so! They like to be known for their ideas – the more complicated the better. They're always thinking of new or different ways of addressing the problem at hand.

***The downside of the Steamroller:*** For a Steamroller, it's all about competence. Unfortunately, there are varying degrees of competence in the world, so I wonder what they say in actual rocket science labs! It's difficult to keep a Steamroller constantly stimulated intellectually. And while they can fill ballrooms with ideas, Steamrollers often get bored thinking through the details, so many of their ideas go unimplemented.

## Are you a Steamroller?

- ☐ I want to be known for my ideas.
- ☐ I think I know it all.
- ☐ I need to be respected.
- ☐ I need to be seen as the subject matter expert.

- ☐ I like to offer my opinions.
- ☐ I can be arrogant.
- ☐ I value education, intellect and competence.
- ☐ I have difficulty giving simple answers.
- ☐ I like to complicate things – it makes it more interesting.
- ☐ I see the endless possibilities – I like to explore.
- ☐ I operate from my gut.
- ☐ I can be argumentative.
- _____ **Total number of checks**

## The Popeye Syndrome

It turns out that my boyfriend's reaction to my original comment about self-awareness leading to transformation was totally predictable. In my years as a management consultant, I've consistently heard the same, "Who, me?" reaction from managers.

Recently, I was in a meeting with about 35 "rough and tumble" senior-level managers and executives discussing the importance of "self-awareness." One of the senior executives obviously thinking that discussing personality types and how to manage different types of people was a complete waste of time, stood up and stated, "Look, this is all fine, well and good – but I am who I am and I'm not going to change." There was dead silence in the training room – then everyone started to look at me! I turned to him and blurted, "Who are you? Popeye the Sailor Man?!" The group laughed, and thankfully, so did the executive.

But unfortunately, there is nothing funny about what I call The Popeye Syndrome – "I yam what I yam, and that's all that I yam…." Probably a good idea for a cartoon character, but inflexible and insensitive for an executive. I swear, I could fill the

Astrodome if I could give a time-out to every manager I heard say...

> *"How can it be me?"*

> *"I've worked my butt off to get where I am – I can't change now."*

> *"I didn't get to the top by being friends with my subordinates!"*

> *"I've been promoted throughout my career – I must be doing something right."*

> *"Like me or not, take it or leave it, this is who I am. I can't change."*

Oh, but you can. And the proof of it is that you're reading this book. The mere fact that you're open to reading a guide on managing people – especially one from someone as unorthodox as "The Corporate Nanny" – means that you are open to and ready for new ideas. You're ready for a change.

# CHAPTER FOUR

# Who's Playing in Your Playground?

So now that you know how you fit into the Playground Personalities, and you see that change is possible (I know you can do it!), let's talk about everyone else.

The key to successful management is to know who you are managing. That means what their personalities are today, where they're coming from and what they're thinking – and just as important – feeling.

I'm sure you can stop your next staff meeting and ask everyone to take the quick 12-point assessment, but it is not very practical nor leader-like! In most situations, you won't have the time to ask people to take an assessment and debrief the results. Now is the time to start practicing how to assess people – on your feet! Whether it's your boss, peers or staff, you must become an expert at quickly deducing the Playground Personalities of others to experience a stress-free work environment!

As The Corporate Nanny, I do need to give you a word of caution before you start the process. Know that every situation is different – and I mean different. Do not think that you've been in this situation before, therefore, the same personalities will appear again. When you think the scenario is the same, you can bet the farm that there is some obscure difference that will affect the outcome. Remember that everyone is a mix of personalities. The Steamroller may have acted in a certain manner in the situation last week, but this week, her Peacemaker is showing. So, here's what you can expect – the unexpected! People will switch their preferred personalities just when you think you know them!

## The Not-so-Pastoral Pastor

Every Tuesday, the executive director of a religious organization, Tom, composes a letter to his congregation and emails it to Edie, his secretary, so she can edit and distribute the weekly e-newsletter. One Wednesday morning, Edie called Tom to let him know that she had not received his latest letter.

"I sent it to you yesterday, like every Tuesday. You must have missed it in your inbox," Tom shot back rather curtly. Respectfully and quietly, Edie repeated the fact that she hadn't received the letter – and the phone call ended with a harsh "click." Tom raced into his office, not to check to see if he was imagining things, but to prove that he was right – that he had sent it the day before. Upon opening his email program, he was dismayed to find that the letter was in his "Draft" folder, and that he had not emailed it after all. Feeling guilty, he picked up the phone, apologized to Edie and sent the email with no further fanfare.

So what happened? What are the personalities of Tom and Edie? How did each react to the other? Have you been in a similar situation?

Now, take a moment, close the book (remember to mark your place) and reflect on the story.

Welcome back.

Let's analyze the story: First, who (meaning, what Playground Personality) is Tom? He thinks he's right – after all, why wouldn't he have sent the letter when he always sends the letter on Tuesdays? Edie is wrong, or worse, incompetent for not finding the email in her own inbox! His impatience, noted by the tone of his voice and his quick response to her, are the classic responses of a Steamroller.

And Edie? Her respectful tone and calm response when confronted by Tom is the clue to her Playground Personality – a Peacemaker.

But there's a twist, as there usually is. Tom tricked us – once he realized that he made the mistake, his secondary Playground Personality appeared – a Peacemaker!

Although Tom was pretty easy to figure out, Edie was a little more of a challenge. She could have been an Organizer (after all, she is on a schedule – newsletter every Wednesday) – and perhaps that's her secondary personality.

How did you do? As I mentioned before, this isn't rocket science. Determining personalities is about observing, listening, and applying the assessment.

## 1 + 2 + 3 = 6

Yes, it's that simple. It's easy to add up the numbers and see that "6" is pretty obvious. Well, the equation for figuring out the Playground Personalities in your office is the same:

$$Application + Observation + Listening$$
$$= Accurate\ Assessment\ of\ Personalities$$

Six equals success. Use just points 1 and 3? No go. Only use 2 and 3? I don't even want to go there. Anything less than 6 will lead to more problems down the line.

## STEP 1: Applying the Playground Personalities

Applying the 12-point Playground Personality assessments in the previous chapter is a little much when you have to operate in

## STEP 1: Applying the Playground Personalities

### The Peacemaker

Needs to make sure everyone is okay.

Is supportive of and cares about others.

Is loyal to the company and his/her staff.

Does not like conflict.

### The Organizer

Manages by scheduling and creating timelines and lists.

Lives in a highly structured world.

Has a high sense of tradition.

Is extremely reliable and dependable.

### The Revolutionary

Hates routine and prefers to act now and beg for forgiveness later.

Is action-oriented and likes to be in the moment.

Is easy to get along with and usually outgoing.

### The Steamroller

Values education, intellect and competence.

Thinks s/he knows it all and needs to be seen as the subject matter expert.

Can be arrogant or argumentative and often operates from the gut.

a flash of managerial genius. So here is a condensed version of the assessment – a Nanny-approved "think on your feet" cheat sheet. This quick list will help to peg the correct personality 80 percent of the time. And as you read on, you will see how the secondary (and sometimes even a third) personality will also affect the outcome of a situation.

But, the list is just part of the process. Keen observation and listening (Steps 2 & 3) will bring your accuracy closer to 95 percent – a respectable gamble to bet your decisions on.

## STEP 2:  Watch Closely...

Have you ever watched your staff? I mean really watched them. Next time, at a larger meeting or in the lunch room, or even from across the room, look at each member of your team. What are they doing? How is her head cocked? Why is he twirling his pen like a baton? What is she writing in the margins of the agenda? Why is he standing so far away from me when we are having a one-on-one conversation?

I could write an entire book on understanding body language in the workplace, but in reality, most interpretation is common sense. However, like other points in this book, relating body language and interactions to each of the Playground Personalities is something you probably haven't put together – another tidbit of Neglected Knowledge.

On the next page is another cheat sheet – this time of behaviors you've probably seen countless times in meetings and interactions.

## STEP 3:  ...And Listen Up

Listening is hard. This is something I had to learn the hard

**STEP 2: Watch Closely...**

| The Peacemaker | The Organizer |
|---|---|
| Eyes dart down in avoidance.<br><br>Squirms in his/her chair or excuses self to the restroom. | Stands up and begins to draw a matrix or schedule on a piece of flipchart paper. |
| **The Revolutionary** | **The Steamroller** |
| Distracted by the whole conversation.<br><br>Doodles or has side conversations with others. | Frowns or holds arms across his/her chest.<br><br>Might try and hijack the meeting. |

way. As a Steamroller, I'm quick to dismiss others' opinions before they are finished being uttered. An ex-boyfriend of mine once told me (on his way out the door) that hearing is physical and passive, but listening is mental and active.

Listening is absorbing the meanings of words and sentences. But listening takes concentration – focusing on the task at hand in spite of distractions. The results are clear – active listening leads to understanding of facts and emotions. The manager who actively listens encourages communication.

For many of you, this is going to be tough. I have to work on it every day – in every interaction – from clients to checkout clerks. But the pay-off is amazing. I am able to understand the subtext – the underlying reality of the situation. When you truly listen, it's like cleaning a window – you might have been able to see before, but when you wipe the haze away, everything is crystal clear.

My third cheat sheet is below. It's short and sweet – and listening for these clues will really help you bring your on-the-fly assessment together.

| STEP 3: ...And Listen Up | |
|---|---|
| **The Peacemaker**<br><br>I feel... | **The Organizer**<br><br>I think... |
| **The Revolutionary**<br><br>I don't like.... | **The Steamroller**<br><br>I believe... |

## How Do You Get to Carnegie Hall?

Practice. It's as simple – and as complicated – as that. You wouldn't know Tom and Edie if you fell over them, but you were able to relate to their story. That's because over time, you have subconsciously learned to recall previous situations, with all of their dealings and results, and quickly apply them to the here-and-now. Now, you need to combine the instant replay model above with the proper application of the Playground Personalities, observation of actions and listening for meanings. That takes patience and practice.

Don't get discouraged. I promise you the first few times you try to listen and observe and apply an assessment – and put it all together – it will feel awkward and not natural. If you try and it doesn't work well, then try again! If you never try you'll never know that you can do it.

Practicing these steps will make you good at what you do. Like the ingredients in those cookies I mentioned a few pages ago, if you forget to add one ingredient to the mixing bowl, you end up with a bitter batter. Using all three steps will give you the comfort that you always have a complete picture of the players. With comfort comes an increased speed in which you can size up your staff. And, the faster you size up your team, the easier it is to remedy any situation. But the only way to improve this skill is to practice – and as any Nanny will remind you, practice makes perfect. Just reading about them in a book is not going to change the way you behave.

## The Nanny Games

The following pages are some of my favorite workplace stories, which I want you to read. After each one, close the book and think about applying the steps you have read about to make your assessment. When you open the book, flip back to this page and I will fill you in on my thoughts.

*Identifying the Personalities*
## The Story: Morning Pow Wow

Ted and Kate were working on a project that required real "brain power." They were frustrated at a meeting they had attended and left feeling the project leader was incompetent. They didn't want to be embarrassed at the next meeting, so they decided to get together early the next morning and do some brainstorming about the project.

The next morning, their manager, Roxanne, who was unaware of their meeting, arrived early to "catch up" on some work.

Apparently, Ted and Kate had too much coffee and were having a "lively, loud and fun" discussion when Roxanne arrived at the office. She thought Ted and Kate were arguing, so she burst into the office to find the walls covered in flipcharts and dozens of sticky notes!

"Is everything all right? Are you guys fighting? I heard shouting from the hallway!" she asked with concern.

Ted and Kate both laughed and replied, "No, we're just brainstorming!"

*A Nanny Challenge*

So what personalities are Ted, Kate and Roxanne? Close the book to think about it. When you have an answer, come back to the book to confirm your thoughts.

*Identifying the Personalities*
## Results: Morning Pow Wow

Ted and Kate appear to be a combination of Steamrollers and Revolutionaries. Thinking that someone is incompetent is a dead give-away to a Steamroller. Also, not wanting to be embarrassed at a meeting – shows signs of the Steamroller personality. But like I said earlier – there can be a change in personality depending upon the situation. And here it comes – as Revolutionaries they work outside of the system – meeting on their own to accomplish what they believe should have been on the project manager's agenda. They didn't get support from their superior. Instead of working with Roxanne, they venture on their own.

Although little is heard from Roxanne, she appears to be a Peacemaker. This is expressed by her concern about the noise from the office, and her offer to break up a possible disagreement. There are subtle clues in her dialogue, which would probably be easier to identify in person than on paper.

*Identifying the Personalities*

## The Story: It's All Greek to Her

The office manager, Margaret, stopped by the office of Sarah, the newly hired executive assistant to the CEO of a medical firm, to say good morning. Margaret noticed that Sarah looked like she was both frustrated and hurt.

When Margaret asked her if something was wrong, Sarah opened up: Stan, her boss, was to give a talk at a prestigious event in Italy, and he asked her to make the travel arrangements – the first time she was given this responsibility. When Sarah started researching flight times, she tried to match them to the event times but got stuck due to the many options. Knowing that Stan is picky about his travel arrangements, she made a list of questions and went into Stan's office anticipating quick answers.

"Do you want to fly to Rome on Monday or Tuesday?" Sarah started to run down her list. She saw that Stan was getting agitated as she continued.

"What do you think? When does the event start? What happens if the plane is late? How much time will it take to get to the hotel?" Stan shot back.

Sarah was so overwhelmed she quietly picked up her pad and excused herself from the office.

After hearing how the events unfolded, Margaret felt compelled to go into Stan's office and organize a meeting to "smooth things over."

Margaret started the meeting by explaining to Stan that all Sarah wanted was a few answers to some travel questions. Stan apologized and explained that while teaching in medical school, he won accolades for his use of the Socratic Method of teaching – a style he adopted for working with his staff.

Sarah appreciated Stan's apology, but looked perplexed as she and Margaret left the office. Picking up on her confusion, Margaret explained that the Socratic Method was about asking questions to discover the truth, rather than just telling what was needed. Sarah understood the explanation – but still didn't know if Stan wanted to fly on Monday or Tuesday!

*A Nanny Challenge*

So what personalities are Sarah, Margaret and Stan? Don't look at the results! Think about it. When you have an answer, come back to the book to confirm your thoughts.

*Identifying the Personalities*
## Results:  It's All Greek to Her

There are some definite clues here:  When someone's feelings get hurt, you can almost determine right away that they are Peacemakers.  Not too many Steamrollers get their "feelings hurt" or if they do, they don't admit it!  Sarah was hesitant to go into Stan's office alone, but seemed willing to have a meeting when Margaret, the Organizer, set it up.  Margaret did a good job at facilitating the dialogue with Stan – although Sarah's questions were still not answered.  And then there's Stan – probably easiest to identify in this story – a Steamroller.  If you watch any type of medical or hospital shows on TV these days – you can see many of the doctors are Steamrollers with a second playground personality that follows right away – a doctor with a "bedside manner" is probably a Steamroller/Peacemaker; a doctor who is in charge of a specific department is probably a combination Steamroller/Organizer; and a doctor who is in charge of the ER is probably a combination Steamroller/Revolutionary.

So you see, you can even observe behavior on TV shows and start to practice the skill of assessing Playground Personalities!

*Identifying the Personalities*

## The Story:  Managing the Manager's Guide

Paul, a human resources manager for a large corporation, is smart, creative and able to put together vast, complex projects. During his workday, Paul was receiving repetitive calls with questions on some of the HR policies, so he decided to write a "Manager's Guide to HR" Handbook and distribute it to all 2,000 managers. Although this was no small task, Paul had been with the company for many years and knew the HR policies inside and out – better than anyone else in his department.

Well, as with other large projects, the handbook began to grow tentacles – other managers wanted their department's information in the book. Soon, the work he thought he was doing independently began to turn into a group project – complete with managing competing personalities. Paul quickly became frustrated and decided he would "stay the course" – his course – and not allow anyone to interfere. After all, it was his idea and his handbook! Paul compiled all of the information and put the book together. When he finished, he thought, "Wow, I'm glad that's done – now we can roll it out!"

He brought the completed handbook to Connie, his manager, for her approval. While she was thrilled the book was completed, she wanted to review and edit it. A week later she delivered her comments – each page came back with painful, detailed edits, questions, suggestions – after all, Connie was a former English teacher. She informed Paul that the handbook looked great, but he needed to contact other departments in the company to verify their policies and finalize their sections.

Paul believed that the other departments already had sufficient time to plan, write and edit their sections of the handbook; therefore, he didn't think he had to go back and ask for additional information. Instead, he only made the edits Connie had wanted him to make.

The next day, Connie was in a meeting with Janet, a peer HR manager to Paul, and told her she was appreciative that Janet took the time to give her policies to Paul for the handbook, and that with her clarified points the book would be a huge success. When Connie asked if Paul had contacted her, Janet curtly replied, "no." Janet didn't share with Connie her thoughts about the handbook, and her resentment that she was not consulted on the project in the first place. She felt that Paul created a project she should have been involved with, didn't like to be told to make edits to her work and didn't believe she was required to cooperate – so she didn't.

After that meeting, Janet accosted Paul, and the two had a verbal altercation. To remedy the situation, Connie called a meeting with Paul and Janet, and asked if they could work together to complete the handbook collaboratively. Connie stated there was enough work for everyone, and she would appreciate them putting their differences aside so that the handbook could be finalized. Reluctantly, they did, and the handbook was distributed to all 2,000 managers.

*A Nanny Challenge*

Identifying Paul, Janet and Connie's primary personality should be a little easier now – but what about their secondary personalities? What else drives them to their actions?

*Identifying the Personalities*

## Results: Managing the Manager's Guide

There is a lot of action in this story – and it is a pretty typical scene in most workplaces. But, as you hone your skills and really understand the Playground Personalities, identifying the players should be getting a little easier.

All of these examples (and 99.9 percent of your staff) share one thing in common – they definitely use one personality. Whatever the situation might bring – creative, collaborative, fraught with conflict – people come to it with the same primary personality every time.

This last story also involved some subtle clues which confirm the primary Playground Personality and then some other clues that describe secondary personalities. Let's see how these expressed themselves through the actions and words of our characters.

Paul is a classic Steamroller. There are the obvious patterns: clever and smart, taking ownership, not thinking he needs to consult others. But let's dig a little deeper. Believing that a task is a "piece of cake" or "not a big deal" is a clue that the person you are working with is probably a Steamroller. Remember my "not rocket science" comment earlier in the book? Steamrollers truly believe that unless they are trying to find a cure for a disease, everything else is pretty much a "no brainer."

In addition, Paul's Revolutionary personality also comes through by his actions. By not wanting to deal with department processes, and thinking that he could single-handedly roll out the handbook, Paul shows some anti-establishment tendencies.

Connie really tries to facilitate the relationships of her staff because she wants everyone to get along. She is a perfect Peacemaker. These relationships are more important than the work.

For Connie, it's not necessarily about the handbook development, but it is about how people work together. How can people work together more effectively? How can she foster open communication? All of these matter to a Peacemaker.

The numerous and meticulous edits Connie makes to the handbook might indicate that her secondary personality is the Organizer. By creating detailed notes (lists), Connie believes that she has set the stage for Paul to succeed.

And then there's Janet. She is upset – but neither to the point of tears, nor to the frustration of, "I'll tear your head off." Instead, she is upset that she had not been consulted – an insult to her intelligence. Steamroller, all the way. She might be less aggressive in her manner than Paul, but when they have a verbal sparring match, the level playing field is clearer.

The fact that Janet reluctantly agreed to work on the handbook with Paul seems to indicate that she also is a Peacemaker. Collaborating for Steamrollers requires them to check their egos at the door – not a simple request. Those Steamrollers who do acquiesce usually have a little Peacemaker in them – somewhere. Even Paul.

# CHAPTER FIVE

# The Complexity of Respect

**How we say it, and how we play it**

We all want to be treated with respect – I cannot imagine anyone who doesn't. But what is respect? It's easy to use the words "I respect you," "Let's treat this problem respectfully," "I demand respect!" But when asked to define the concept, many people cannot articulate their interpretation.

Respect means many different things. It can mean taking someone's feelings, needs, thoughts, ideas, wishes and preferences into serious consideration – and giving them worth and value. We express this through acknowledgment, listening, truthfulness and acceptance.

But this definition is mine. Your definition might vary considerably – and not surprisingly – primarily based on your Playground Personality. Later on, I will discuss how each personality views and shows respect, but first we need to tackle a few basics.

**Respect goes hand-in-hand with communication.** If communication in your office is out of alignment, you can bet that respect issues will surface. A classic example: A staff member's work is harshly addressed by a manager without a clear understanding of each other's side of the issue. The staff member believes that management does not respect his/her work; and management believes that the staff member does not respect his/her authority.

**Respect starts at home – with you.** You must understand how others view respect, and you must show yours in return in an appropriate manner. If respect is absent in the workplace, then it's going to be really hard for you, as the manager, to accomplish your goals and for your staff to understand what's needed to keep the work flowing.

I remember taking questions at a training I held at a large transportation company. Staff complained that the management team did not show them respect. They were hard pressed to come up with examples, but their feeling was strong.

During the break, I was walking through the bus depot when I noticed two drivers violently arguing at the gas pumps. Concerned that a fight was imminent, I carefully approached them and asked, "Hey guys, what's up?"

Bob told me he was late and needed to get out of the lot first so he could keep to his schedule. Sam, the other driver, didn't seem to care that Bob was running late – so he continued to fill his tank. I asked both if they thought it was respectful to argue with each other. I ended by saying, "If you want management to respect you, don't you think you have to respect each other first?"

I later heard that the incident was reported back to the transportation manager (not by me), and that issues began to be addressed and attitudes started to change.

I've had my share of refereeing arguments, and not just between staff – but between executives, too!

**Respect is primal.** The foundation of our psychological need to feel respected traces its roots back to the beginning of time. A person who was thought to have no worth, importance or value to our nomadic ancestors could be left behind, and would most likely perish.

Scientists are learning that even animals need to be treated with respect. Recent studies show that dogs are capable of feeling jealousy (a lack of respect) towards one another – and their trainers – when one is rewarded and another is not. On a recent trip to Sea World, I remember one of the animal trainers telling the crowd, "At Sea World, we don't 'tell' our animals what do to – we 'ask' them!" I really took that to heart, thinking, "Wow, if we could only adopt that philosophy in the workplace."

**The principles of respect never change, but the ways we express it do.** The virtue of respect has recently been challenged by technology – most notably how we use emails to communicate with our staff. I once read that, with the exceptions of handguns and tequila, no invention has ever caused so many problems in less time than a computer. With cell phones, mobile devices, instant messaging, video chat, texts and emails – we are always "on." We must always be aware of how others receive our words and gestures, whether in person or through technology.

I was interrupted at work by a loud bellow from one of my staff members, Ted, as he ran into my office waving a piece of paper in his hand. Ted had a look of sheer horror on his face, so I couldn't imagine what had happened. He sat down, shoved the paper in my face and blurted, "Here, read this!" I read the first sentence and thought, "Oh no, here we go!"

The printout included a series of emails between Ben, a senior director in the firm, and Mike in engineering. Mike sent the original email to notify Ben that a specific decision had been made on a large project. Ben fired back an email expressing his discontent about the decision, stating that Mike "was a moron for allowing that decision to be made." As if that wasn't bad enough, Mike also forwarded Ben's email to the entire Engineering Department – 40 people. You see where this is going?

Ted received the email string from a member of the engineering staff who was very upset and couldn't believe that Ben could be so insensitive. The staff member wanted the issue immediately addressed by HR (by the way, HR loves it when we have to get in the middle of these scuffles!). I wished Ben would have expressed himself differently – but he hadn't – and a plan to placate emotions was put into action.

I called Ben into my office to explain the situation and let him know that his email had become infamous when it was forwarded to the entire Engineering Department. At first, Ben did not react. I was curious at this behavior, and finally asked him, "Ben, do you understand why this is a problem?" "No."

I pointed out that it was the use of the word "moron" that had everyone upset. It's safe to say that the word "moron," or any derivative, is offensive and not a good word choice. Before I finished my speech, I could see the blood rush out of Ben's face. "I didn't mean to use it as a noun. I meant to use the word as an adjective — to say that the decision was moronic." Ben returned to his office and immediately sent an apology email to the entire Engineering Department.

## Respect and the Playground Personalities
*Each one plays it a different way*

The complexities of gaining, showing and maintaining respect become apparent when you look at each of the Playground Personalities. Each of the following sections is rather detailed – but do not worry, for The Corporate Nanny has provided more cheat sheets for your quick reference.

# RESPECT AND THE PEACEMAKER

## How the Peacemaker Shows Respect to Others –
*People are People!*

Peacemakers focus on people – listening to them with un-divided attention, looking into their eyes, responding to their needs and making them feel like they are the most important people in the room. This engaging experience defines respect for a Peacemaker.

Showing respect plays both sides of the Peacemaker's coin: by bolstering up people, they get what they need from them, while at the same time, they make people feel good about them-selves. Peacemakers know that paying attention to others, always being enthusiastic, smiling and making people feel impor-tant – through verbal and non-verbal cues – are the cornerstones of respect. Whether they are working with the janitor or the CEO, Peacemakers treat all people the same. Titles and accolades mean little, because quite simply – people are people!

While some of us are more reserved when we interact with others, Peacemakers subscribe to the theory that everyone enjoys getting attention and appreciates it when others spend time with them. That is one reason Peacemakers make great coaches – they take the time to get to know others, and offer advice or sugges-tions to improve one's life or work.

## How the Peacemaker Encourages Respect from Others –
*Figuring it Out*

Peacemakers encourage respect in the same way they show it – by spending the time to figure out the person, knowing their likes and dislikes, what recharges their batteries, what makes them happy or sad – what makes them tick. This discovery process takes a great deal of time for many, but for the Peacemaker, this ability is natural and automatic. They appreciate when others recognize this innate talent and that it is not a burden, but a necessary part of all relationships. Want to make a Peacemaker's day? Observe their body language, compliment them, make introductions to others in front of them and make sure people receive the resources they need to be productive and happy.

## How the Peacemaker Perceives Disrespect – *No more sharing!*

Peacemakers never openly disrespect others. They know that their personalities can be taken over by stronger personalities, and that they, perhaps, can be easily manipulated. Their intense need to please people and help others sometimes brings on disrespect from co-workers. They know that can happen, and they are always looking ahead in order to avoid unnecessary confrontations.

Make no mistake; Peacemakers can completely lose all respect for individuals. Outwardly, they will be polite and civil, but inside, the truth is well known. When Peacemakers begin to not share personal information, withdraw their attention or do not smile or laugh – that is a clear signal that they have lost respect for you. They are rarely ever directly accused of being disrespectful, since on appearance, they act in a respectful manner – to keep the peace at all costs. But the cost of this internal turmoil is substantial. Peacemakers usually have to deal with physical reactions to their emotional state, such as feeling sick to their stomachs or becoming exhausted. More often than not, these physical reactions will turn into real illness. It's an upsetting situation to be in – Peacemakers just want to be friendly towards others – even if it means hurting themselves if the outcomes go against their nature.

Ways to lose the respect of Peacemakers? Ignore them, discount someone else's opinion, mock a co-worker, curse or use condescending language towards others – and a big one – report an issue to a superior without consulting the Peacemaker first.

## Is the Peacemaker's Respect Forever?

Peacemakers give you a few chances to earn their respect – with a big caveat. Peacemakers believe in the benefit of the doubt. Whatever caused them to disrespect someone in the first place may have changed. Because of this, people may get back into a Peacemaker's good graces. However, if you blow your second chance (or third or fourth), the respect is damaged. The more times you cross Peacemakers, the less respect they will show with each subsequent reconciliation – until there is no respect to be had. In that case, Peacemakers will go out of their way to avoid working with these people altogether.

Peacemakers believe everyone is the same – show them otherwise, and you will lose their trust. That is not to say they cannot work with you. Unlike other Playground Personalities, Peacemakers can work with people they disrespect. They will do so in a professional and civil manner, but they'll never give you the respect or trust they initially did.

## Things to Consider

Peacemakers rarely lose their cool. If someone is off track, they gently reveal the facts about what is going on in the situation, often asking others for their side of the story and putting a plan in place to work out a solution together.

Unless people are completely lost on task, Peacemakers don't tell them what to do. They do their best to get the buy-in from others, so the ownership of responsibility is transferred to that person. They feel that if a person comes up with an idea on their own – they'll follow through with it.

It's all about collaboration for Peacemakers – getting each person's ideas and trying to make them work for everyone. They like to make sure everyone's opinions and ideas are heard, and they facilitate the group to make sure this happens.

Peacemakers put a great deal of emphasis on the art of compromise. If a conflict arises, they will calm down those involved, choose their words carefully and give full credit where credit is due! Peacemakers would never disrespect someone's idea – even

---

*The Nanny Cheat Sheet:* **Respect and the Peacemaker**

| How a Peacemaker shows respect: | How to show a Peacemaker respect: |
|---|---|
| Focuses on the person. Peacemakers value personal contact and relationships. | Work collaboratively, brainstorm ideas and get people involved along the way! |
| **What is disrespect?** Ignoring or mocking someone – Heaven forbid cursing! | **Can respect be repaired?** Yes, but returns diminish with each reconciliation. |

though they may not think it's a good one. Instead, they may offer an alternative idea or give others a chance to try it their way.

Peacemakers are always "in the moment" when they are with their staff or a group. They are not distracted by ringing phones, beeping emails or vibrating PDAs. It is the utmost disrespect not to give their full attention to whatever they are doing at the moment – especially while in a meeting or working on a project.

## RESPECT AND THE ORGANIZER

### How the Organizer Shows Respect to Others –
*Squeezing out a "thank you"*

If you work for an Organizer, don't expect hugs or even pats on the back. For an Organizer, showing respect is implied. When a coworker does a good job, or if someone accomplishes a task, the work will get recognition. Organizers aren't going to fall all over people with gushy or gooey sentiments – in fact the acknowledgments are very subtle. Organizers will simply state they are happy that the work is done, possibly adding a "great job" for good measure. For the Organizer, it's all about getting things done – not necessarily recognizing the people who did the work!

"Thank you" doesn't come naturally for Organizers. This is not a sign of rudeness, but a matter-of-fact belief that people are there to work, and are paid to do so. Accomplishing tasks is the primary goal of work. And while Organizers usually have to go out of their way to thank someone, they do – although it might sound more like, "I'm glad you organized this project, and knew all the work that had to be done before you started. Now it's done!" Not as melodic or simple as "thank you," but in their heart, the sentiment is the same.

Remember, Organizers lead their lives by lists – you shouldn't be surprised to see the item "Thank Staff" on their master To-Do list. They usually reflect on things they have to do either before they leave work for the day or in the morning when they arrive. Organizers are satisfied when they get things done – and that satisfaction translates into respect.

## How the Organizer Encourages Respect from Others – *The busier the better*

Organizers encourage respect in the same way they show it – when things get done. Organizers like to be tasked with projects – not just busy work – but work with meaningful implications. And they love deadlines. Being asked to complete a project without a deadline will usually lead them to create their own timelines, killing themselves in the process only to hear, "Oh, I didn't expect this for at least another week."

The old adage "give work to busy people" rings true for Organizers. In their minds, busy people have important things going on. In the event of a lull in their workload, an Organizer will call a meeting and ask around the table, "What's on your list that you have been trying to do, but haven't been able to, because you've been so busy?" Once they collect this information, they will sort through the answers and start people working on the new projects! In the eyes of an Organizer, there is always something that needs to be done.

## How the Organizer Perceives Disrespect – *"Don't roll your eyes at me"*

Organizers feel disrespected when someone insults their work. In their mind, it's okay for people not to like them – but people need to appreciate their work. If the insult is out of character for them, if they have never received that specific feedback before or if the insult comes from someone they don't respect to begin with, often times, the Organizer will become downright angry. This anger turns into an unbelievable drive to be successful, or to disprove that person's opinion about the Organizer's ability to get things done.

Organizers also pick up on non-verbal cues which could lead them to believe that they have been disrespected, including the showing of anger, rolling eyes, walking away or slamming drawers.

Organizers don't go out of their way to disrespect others; however, they do subscribe to the theory "an eye for an eye." If a staff member disrespects an Organizer, he or she might turn around and be disrespectful in retaliation.

## Yours – or not – forever

Basically, Organizers are loyal with regard to respect – once you are respected, they will be faithful for life. However, in the event of a breach in consideration – being "played," breaking a confidence, lying to them or trying to pull the wool over their eyes – their respect is gone. And, once an Organizer declares it gone – it's gone – and it can never be repaired. There aren't too many absolutes in life, but for the Organizer, this is one of them. In all of my years, I have never known an Organizer to take someone back after s/he was disrespected!

## Walking the floors, owning your task and getting it done

For the Organizer, showing people respect by "walking the floors" is very important. That means you don't go straight from the elevator door to your office to get ready for the day without greeting people. Organizers may have to build this into their list, but one way or another, they won't forget it!

Organizers use their resources wisely. They pride themselves in knowing their staff's likes and strengths, and if they believe someone is good at a particular task, Organizers will go out of their way to assign them that work. Using resources wisely is part of getting things done, checking off lists and feeling a sense of accomplishment.

---

*The Nanny Cheat Sheet:* **Respect and the Organizer**

| How an Organizer shows respect: | How to show an Organizer respect: |
|---|---|
| Comments on your work. Organizers value the quality of personal work habits. | Assign meaningful work with specific deadlines and tasks to the Organizer. |
| **What is disrespect?** | **Can respect be repaired?** |
| Calling in an expert when the Organizer has the expertise. Impatience. Taking a task, then not completing it. | Never — so don't cross an Organizer! |

Organizers believe that adults should be able to work out their differences and resolve problems or issues that may arise. They respect their staff and managers by making it a safe environment and providing a forum for that to happen. Accepting the invitation to put something on the table is a key way to show respect to an Organizer. This ownership of tasks is central. Complaining that work was not completed because of a staff conflict is not acceptable to Organizers. They reward people for getting the work done. Having the staff get along while working is an extra benefit.

Assessing personalities is not a natural process for Organizers. Knowing this, they believe that the key to getting work done through others is to communicate the way they would like to have people communicate with them. Organizers have learned to tailor their communications to each individual, because they want everyone to be successful.

## RESPECT AND THE REVOLUTIONARY

### How the Revolutionary Shows Respect to Others – *The Wild Ride*

I was having lunch with a Revolutionary friend of mine and asked her, "When you show or give respect – what does it look like?" In typical Revolutionary fashion, she shot back, "Let me tell you what disrespect looks like!" I laughed so loud, the whole restaurant glared at us.

Revolutionaries show – or gain – respect (leave it to a Revolutionary to make a different word choice) by taking people for who and what they are, respecting people for working hard and giving credit to people who try something new – even if it doesn't work. When Revolutionaries take others on their "wild rides," the result is usually positive. In fact, Revolutionaries don't ask people to ride along unless they are respected to begin with. Once a high level of respect and trust is established, most people enjoy being with a Revolutionary – it is fun, and you never know where you'll end up!

Generally, Revolutionaries can be counted on to handle "the stuff that no one else wants to handle." While they don't like people getting in their way, they do respect people who offer to help – especially if they are in the middle of a crisis and time is of the essence. They gain respect through their actions. Revolutionaries always remember to celebrate the successes of others on their team. An excuse to have some fun is in the soul of every Revolutionary – needless to say, there's always a celebration going on!

## How the Revolutionary Encourages Respect from Others – *Mission Impossible*

Revolutionaries feel most respected when they are called in to work on non-routine projects – or better yet – when there's a "mission impossible" event. The more challenging the project, the better! Revolutionaries work best when the project involves unsolved mysteries, emergencies or any event that calls for someone to work in a situation where the outcome is unknown. They feel a rush by not knowing all the details – doing the "detective work" to figure things out is a huge reward. This Playground Personality likes a lot of action. They know when someone rings them and says, "We called you to help us because you are the best," they translate that to "They called me because no one else would handle this mess!" And, Revolutionaries love to get others involved, because they know they can't do the impossible on their own!

## How the Revolutionary Perceives Disrespect –
### *"I was just kidding!"*

Revolutionaries feel disrespected when they "get in trouble" for being playful and their comments or actions are misconstrued. They don't like to be "called on the carpet" to explain what they said or did.

As is often the case, Revolutionaries get caught up in the moment, and an offhand comment could innocently hurt someone's feelings or show disrespect. Most of the time, they don't even remember what transpired in the situation, and they certainly don't go out of the way to upset someone!

Their love for action is a double-edged sword. Often, Revolutionaries don't think before they speak, because they only want to get an idea out before they forget it – which often causes them to want to eat their words. The old proverb, "There is a time and place for everything," is something they never learned in school. Or choose not to remember.

Revolutionaries are people oriented and are sometimes labeled disrespectful if they are looking out for their own self-interests and not the interests of the team or the organization. They may be competent in what they do, but if they don't have others supporting them – in other words, are insular, not team oriented – they will lose respect at all levels. Having people skills is really important for this Playground Personality.

## Is the Revolutionary's Respect Forever?

Often for a Revolutionary, respect comes and goes depending upon the person and the situation. First, a Revolutionary must give it – and then they must work hard to keep it. Once a Revolutionary gives respect, it's not absolute that it will last. This is the Playground Personality that "walks the talk" in order to gain and retain respect. It's not just about words – it's really about watching and observing.

If a Revolutionary doesn't recognize that the things they say or do impacts everyone around them, they will have trouble maintaining others' respect. A Revolutionary may be good at their trade, but when they are perceived as unprofessional, the respect can easily be broken.

A Revolutionary truly believes that you are only as good as your last project, and will give respect based on your most recent actions. When a Revolutionary gives respect, it can easily be taken back.

## Things to Consider

Courtesy is at the center of the Revolutionary personality. They often use basic "respect" tactics at work – saying "Hello" or "Good Morning," and they try to drum up conversations about others' interests – the more "dare-devilish" the better! They make it a point to understand staff job positions. "I remember when I was in charge of dispatch – it was a stressful assignment – but I loved it!" is proof to the staff that they understand the technical aspects of what they do.

Most of all, what sets Revolutionaries apart from the other Playground Personalities is the respect they show to their staff for "getting" the work done. This is very different from the Organizer, who cares about "what" gets done. Revolutionaries are not micro-managers, and they don't hover over cubicle walls to make sure their staff is working. They let the staff work independently. Staff members know the Revolutionary is there for them if they need help or support – but at the end of the day, the staff is trusted to get the job done.

Usually, Revolutionaries only have to say to the staff "this is what I need you to do," and the staff will run with it! Don't be mistaken – Revolutionaries have to be genuine in the way they treat staff members, such as holding them accountable. They generally do not beat up staff if something goes wrong. They interact with them as professionals and chalk things up to having a bad day if something doesn't work exactly right. Once you gain their respect at work – it becomes a two-way street – you can ask them to do just about anything – and they will perhaps climb a mountain for you!

*The Nanny Cheat Sheet:* **Respect and the Revolutionary**

| How a Revolutionary shows respect: | How to show a Revolutionary respect: |
|---|---|
| Focuses on the situation and the people in it in order to get to a positive solution. | Working on the impossible and doing it with ease and passion. |
| **What is disrespect?** | **Can respect be repaired?** |
| Not taking responsibility and always blaming the other person. | Yes! |

## RESPECT AND THE STEAMROLLER

### How the Steamroller Shows Respect to Others – *The "A" Team*

Steamrollers are all about the bling. Not fancy jewelry, but plaques, awards, letters after their name and title – very visible reflections on status in the workplace. With these nods to credibility comes their respect. To a Steamroller, education is one of the top competence-thresholds for themselves and in judging others – your school, your degree, your accolades are critically important when respecting others. Accepting an invitation to speak at a promotion ceremony or commencement for a notable education institution is the pinnacle sign of respect for a Steamroller.

Along with this need for credibility, Steamrollers need to know that those whom they respect also are respected by others – they don't suffer fools gladly. This is very important when they are building teams and trying to recruit the "best and the brightest." Steamrollers want to be known for putting together the perfect "A" Team!"

When it comes to seeking advice, Steamrollers are selective about whom they seek out or ask to weigh in. They must respect the person who is giving the advice. Unsolicited advice – even from a respected source – is a big turn off.

However, Steamrollers have learned that there is great value in the person who, an hour before a deadline, says, "Let's test this just one more time before we go live!" They may show signs of impatience, but they do appreciate the feedback!

## How the Steamroller Encourages Respect from Others – *Make it Happen!*

Just as Steamrollers need to see credentials – they need to show them off, too. If a Steamroller has an official title or marks of credibility – s/he uses them.

Respect for a Steamroller is in actions and words. Steamrollers are not interested in people just listening to them, but rather, taking their ideas and making something happen! Steamrollers don't want someone placating them – their respect doesn't come into play until something happens. Nothing happens? Then they will go elsewhere, where their ideas will be acted upon – even if that means they do it themselves.

## How the Steamroller Perceives Disrespect – *Fight to the Bitter End*

It's hard for Steamrollers to feel disrespected – at least in their minds. But when they do, it is usually because they believe others think their competency is in question. Steamrollers react to disrespect by fighting to the bitter end to prove the other guy wrong – or just writing that person off. They can take the heat, and know how to give it back – and they won't go down without a fight – public or private!

Steamrollers lose respect for people who have goals they don't achieve, or dreams that aren't fulfilled. For them, it's not about the time spent on this planet – but what they accomplished for the greater good.

## Is the Steamroller's Respect Forever?

Once a Steamroller gives respects, it is usually for good, unless the person violates the respect – either directly with the

Steamroller or with someone else. As I mentioned before, when a Steamroller loses respect in you, you are taken off the list.

While Steamrollers can have respect for a profession, but not respect the person in that job, depending on the level of infraction, they also may question that person's profession – or even the whole industry.

## Things to Consider

Steamrollers like to teach concepts to the staff, and feel respected when they are listened to. Explaining the "big picture," telling the staff of a project's importance and showing the staff how to make it all happen are ways a Steamroller shows respect in a day-to-day manner.

While many Steamrollers recognize that not everyone has the same background or level of expertise, they do expect that staff members are productive and work accurately. When this does not happen, they change their strategy from teaching to showing. While this might be annoying to others, it beats the alternative of jumping up and down in frustration!

While Steamrollers may lose respect in the eyes of others over one of their tantrums, they give respect to others who do not exhibit the same behavior when they are frustrated. They highly respect those who do not disrespect others for not having a higher level of understanding, but try their best.

Steamrollers like to do things their way and rarely take feedback or suggestions. Remember, when you had a substitute teacher in school and you didn't like the way s/he did something? You would question their authority with, "That's not how Miss Smith does it…." The usual reply was, "Well this is how I do it!" – a classic Steamroller response.

My boyfriend has since dubbed this the "Miss Smith

Syndrome." Steamrollers find it difficult to entertain new and improved ways of working. Showing respect to the staff often means allowing them to offer different ways of completing tasks – and for the Steamroller to truly listen. If and when they decide to change the process, Steamrollers will go out of their way to recognize the people who made the change happen.

---

*The Nanny Cheat Sheet:* **Respect and the Steamroller**

| How a Steamroller shows respect: | How to show a Steamroller respect: |
|---|---|
| Calls in the resident expert for help with a problem. | Give them a difficult problem to solve and ask for their opinions. |
| **What is disrespect?** | **Can respect be repaired?** |
| Using someone's idea without giving them credit! | Maybe it can be earned back once it's lost. |

---

*A Nanny Challenge*

**The Story: The Battling Emails**

Okay, now it is time to turn this complicated concept into a practical reality. Remember the story of the email incident in the Engineering Department? Ted, Ben and Mike – and even I – are all very different Playground Personalities in this story. Close the book, and take a moment to analyze the situation. When you have an answer, come back to the book to confirm your thoughts.

## Results: The Battling Emails

We've got lots of Steamrollers here – Ben and Mike for starters. When an email, or any communication for that matter, comes as a surprise to the recipient, the sender is probably a Steamroller! Remember, Steamrollers don't think they have to explain themselves and believe that people should just take the information given to them and move on. But when a Steamroller (Mike) sent an email to another Steamroller (Ben) – sparks began to fly! So when Ben fired the email back about the whole "moron" thing, Mike in turn wanted to destroy his credibility – so he sent it to everyone in the department.

In this situation, Ted was the Peacemaker. He was upset and disappointed about the email trail and wanted to acknowledge the staff and how they were unfairly misrepresented.

I was using all of my Playground Personalities. My Revolutionary read the email trail and picked up the phone without getting all of the facts. My Organizer started to collect facts once I knew Ben was coming to my office. My Peacemaker tried to facilitate Ben's understanding of why Mike got upset in the first place. And, my Steamroller went for the jugular when I sternly said, "Don't use any form of the word "moron!" And trust me – for a Steamroller, only speaking sternly is restrained.

# CHAPTER SIX

# Facing Facts

**You *Can* Handle the Truth**

I don't subscribe to the proverb "no news is good news." Instead, a more practical version – and the one that usually keeps me out of trouble – is "no news is bad news." Think about it. We all know that bad news travels fast, but if you had a "heads up" on a situation before it turned ugly, wouldn't you try to fix it before it had the chance to spiral out of control?

If you are as impatient as I am, facing facts can be a long and painful ordeal. That is why most managers ignore them, thinking, "If I don't deal with this today, hopefully it will be gone tomorrow!" If only wishing away problems worked. Not facing facts has profound implications on both people and processes.

Facing facts – finding and acknowledging the awful truth – takes time and energy, can be an unpleasant process and makes others uncomfortable – all which make it difficult. There is always something preventing us from taking the time to do it well, and most of us are easily distracted from the task. But, you can't collect them alone – you need the help of your staff. Without conquering this critical skill – possibly the most basic of "The Forgotten Five" – you will always be left wondering if you have all the facts.

## Different Ideas on the Truth

Getting to the bottom of the story is not as simple as it may seem. How reliable are the people telling you the facts? Are their opinions sprinkled in? Are important facts left out because they are afraid to get themselves or someone else in trouble? Did you really ask for their take on the issue in the first place?

These are all important points to consider while you're fact gathering, and all tie into the previous chapter about understanding respect. It's difficult to inquire about the truth of a situation – especially if you don't know the Playground Personality of the person you are dealing with – or their perceptions of respect.

Until analyzing people's Playground Personalities and understanding their perceptions on respect become second nature, you might have to consciously take steps to make sure you have collected enough facts. But, when this skill becomes more natural – and it will – you'll fly through the process with the greatest of ease, without even being aware that you're doing it!

Even as an "old pro," I find myself running through all of my Playground Personalities to get at the facts. I will start with my Organizer – I love details, facts and straight answers, even if they are hard to swallow. Next, I validate information along the way, so the facts aren't so overwhelming – my Steamroller. Of course, I like to discover issues way in advance of anything exploding, which taps into my Revolutionary. Finally, and sometimes the hardest one for me to remember, is that facing facts is not just about the process, but also about how people come into the picture – the core of the Peacemaker.

## Treading Toward Disaster: The Third Wheel

The executive director of a nonprofit organization, Jim, had a pool of three administrative secretaries in his department. Jill and Delores had been with the organization for many years, while Tricia was only recently hired.

Tricia was brought into the organization during a very turbulent time, and she did not receive an appropriate orientation.

Jim never took the time to "show her the ropes," so she wasn't exactly sure of her duties and responsibilities; therefore, she always felt unprepared for the job. Jill and Delores liked Tricia and tried as much as they could to help her along, but they had their own work to do. In any case, it was no substitute for a proper orientation.

Because of Tricia's lack of preparedness and understanding of her responsibilities, over the course of a few months, tension and friction started growing in the office. When Delores finally approached Jim about the situation, he sternly responded, "You are all grown-ups. Manage yourselves and get along."

Weeks passed, and the situation did not improve. Tricia began to feel like an outsider as Jill and Delores treated her as though she was incompetent, and bad feelings began to fester. All the while Jim knew of the situation, but didn't have the time or the inclination to address the issues. Finally, Tricia made a costly mistake, and Jim didn't take the news well – he blew up at Tricia and made her cry.

I'm sure you have already figured out the Playground Personalities (you are getting so good at this!). But what are the facts in this story?

The office was going through change; a new staff person was hired and expected to pick up the work with no training; there was minimal interaction with Jim; a plea for help was ignored; and a mistake was made.

Jim (Steamroller) didn't face the facts, didn't make time to handle the "office issues" and just wanted everyone to get along. Jill, Delores and Tricia (Peacemakers) wanted to get along and get their work done. If Jim had taken time to address the facts and try to facilitate the staff, the outcome would have been very different. Instead, ignoring the facts made for an unpleasant outcome.

*Here's a quick Nanny Tip:* If you ever hear yourself responding to a plea for help with, "Work it out," know that you have begun your decline down a slippery slope, because you probably don't have all the facts. Stop. Assess. Find out what's going on before a mistake is made.

## Facts and the Playground Personalities

Finding the facts requires you to evaluate how each Playground Personality faces facts. After each of the following, The Corporate Nanny has provided more cheat sheets to help you collect your facts.

## FACTS AND THE PEACEMAKER

### It's All About the Non-Verbal Cues

In order to find the truth, Peacemakers must speak to people face-to-face. This is intentional, as they personally choose those who they want to question – those they see as "insightful." This insight is found in the body language of the interviewee. Peacemakers have the ability to easily see past the words and actions of others and gain a better and deeper perspective about people through their non-verbal cues. In fact, meeting with people face-to-face is critical, because they can match the person's body language with what they hear. If the pieces don't match, Peacemakers will continue to probe until they feel comfortable with the facts. They are constantly watching for cues, because they don't want to miss something.

Peacemakers try to collect facts from every side of the situation, because they appreciate that people may view things differently. They spend a great deal of time preparing questions and meeting with people who often have a perspective that's different from theirs. Peacemakers will spend extra time collecting facts if the situation will eventually affect the well-being of a person or entire department. Remember, Peacemakers show respect by including people and making them feel included.

Peacemakers are afraid to ignore new facts as they come into play, because they may miss something. They will try to enhance their knowledge of the new facts by searching for more information, and they will attempt to collect facts from leadership groups or "people who influence others."

There's a delicate balance between "heart" and "head" for Peacemakers. They will analyze the situation with both logic and emotion, asking. "Are these the facts I need?" It is a very conscious effort, and both the heart and head must be in synch. The logical facts have to be clear, and their heart has to validate them. That is why, when faced with an unpleasant truth, Peacemakers will believe the validity of the information – after all, why else would co-workers go out of their way to tell them in the first place? This is also why Peacemakers are able to extract information from people who are usually difficult to ask – because in their hearts, they know they can walk away from the situation with some tidbit of fact.

When Peacemakers find out that the information they received was incorrect, they may be thrown for a loop. Because they are very trusting, they assume people will be honest with them from the start. The idea that someone would have a hidden agenda would never cross their mind, so if someone intentionally gives Peacemakers the wrong facts, they will become upset. This will also lead them to reconsider other facts they have received and become suspicious that future facts will be false, also. Peacemakers will go back to the original facts, look at their assumptions and see if they can draw the same conclusions – even if some of the facts are wrong.

Peacemakers subscribe to the ideas of "save face" and "lose face." Depending upon their relationship with the interviewee, and how the facts affect the interviewee personally, the Peacemaker believes people are entitled to know that their facts were wrong – helping that person to "save face." On the other hand, why place blame on the person who gave them the wrong facts. Why hurt their feelings if the facts were not of consequence to them in the first place – why should they "lose face." Telling people they were wrong may inhibit them from helping Peacemakers in the future.

---

*The Nanny Cheat Sheet:* **Facts and the Peacemaker**

| How a Peacemaker collects facts: | How a Peacemaker Finds the Facts: Who does s/he depend on? | Wrong facts and the Peacemaker: |
|---|---|---|
| Through the eyes of others. | Trusted sources – ones s/he likes and doesn't particularly like – but asks anyway. | S/he will figure it out and don't need to point fingers at others. |

## FACTS AND THE ORGANIZER

### It's all about past experiences

When Organizers collect facts, they approach everyone involved in the situation and ask lots of questions based on their experiences. Organizers contact those who have had similar experiences, figuring if someone has done this before, then they should have the facts – basically, a "Been There, Done That" list. Experience over accolades: the person with a master's degree from an Ivy League school is listed well below the high school graduate who has been through this issue before.

Organizers need to speak face-to-face or over the phone, rather than email – the personal connection is key. Typically, they will ask the same initial questions to everyone in hopes of finding a pattern in the replies. Depending on the answers they receive, additional questioning may be necessary. Organizers dislike "yes" or "no" answers, so they usually begin with their own questions, followed by questions based on the answers they receive. Organizers need to ground their questions with research, and like to use professional networks and Internet resources. And, because of their need for efficiency, Organizers can get a little impatient when hunting down people for answers. When an Organizer calls, be prepared!

Organizers will go the extra mile to get closure on the facts – and to cross the items off their lists. They know they are close to the end of the process when they begin to receive consistent information or validation – the facts start to match the situation. Since they do not take things at face value, this consistency and validation is critically important. Organizers need to be aware of their propensity to prematurely check items off their list in anticipation of a certain response.

Organizers become quite upset when they do not receive accurate facts. While on the outside they may appear to brush off the inaccuracy with a glib, "Oh well, I guess this isn't coming off my list," their disappointment will drive them to work even harder. They will to go back and collect more facts – but not from the person who led them astray. They need only to get the facts, fix the problem, look forward and check the item off their lists for their own satisfaction, as the Organizer does not feel the need to prove anyone wrong. And, once the list is all checked off, the issue is "boxed up and shipped out," not to be revisited.

---

*The Nanny Cheat Sheet:* **Facts and the Organizer**

| How an Organizer collects facts: | How an Organizer Finds the Facts: Who does s/he depend on? | Wrong facts and the Organizer: |
|---|---|---|
| As a list that needs to be validated. | People s/he knows who have had similar experiences and by asking lots of questions. | Doesn't mind going back and collecting more facts – but wants closure. |

## FACTS AND THE REVOLUTIONARY

### There's No Substitute for Investigation

When Revolutionaries need to collect facts, they always begin with themselves, followed by the rest of the world! They look to themselves and their experiences to see all of the possibilities of getting from "Point A" to "Point C" even before they start to question others. Their minds imprint an immediate outline of what needs to be done, and they can easily visualize the "10 facts" they need to know about a situation. This step is an automatic response, and is often done in an instant. This quick game plan is all that is needed for them to become grounded before they can begin interviewing others.

With their game plan prepared, they are ready to question everyone from the line staff to the executive level. They know that finding facts is a team effort, and they approach it that way. Revolutionaries need co-patriots, which is why they must tap into the line staff to assist in their investigation.

Revolutionaries will recall from past experiences, projects or situations they have encountered; they'll look through old papers, pull files, use internal resources and research on the Internet. No stone is left unturned!

However, this process can become rather messy, as the Revolutionary collects facts in a random process – often by trial and error. Revolutionaries juggle many different facts that support a variety of scenarios. They want to know all the angles of a situation, and they need to find the facts to back up each angle. This lack of efficiency may impede their ability to extract some information, so they will analyze potential questions that could be asked of them and go back and collect "back-up facts" that would support conflicting points of view. Revolutionaries never want to be in a situation where they don't know all of the facts.

Revolutionaries don't get rattled when they receive information they don't want to hear. They look at it as an opportunity to take a better look at the facts. However, they may get overly concerned that they are missing something and start double-checking items to see if something went wrong.

At the end of the day, Revolutionaries are not afraid to get wrong facts, because they will just shift their plan and search for new information. If, however, someone deliberately gives them misinformation, their heads can "spin off their shoulders!" They will get physically upset and remind the offending informant about the business ramifications of giving bad information. Revolutionaries believe that people give wrong information for two reasons: to stay out of trouble or to sway a decision in their favor. Both are ways to lose a Revolutionary's respect instantly.

| *The Nanny Cheat Sheet:* **Facts and the Revolutionary** | | |
|---|---|---|
| **How a Revolutionary collects facts:**<br><br>Like an investigation. | **How a Revolutionary Finds the Facts: Who does s/he depend on?**<br><br>S/he will ask everyone – s/he puts no filter or screen on the person. | **Wrong facts and the Revolutionary:**<br><br>Doesn't like it – but will continue to search until the search is complete. |

# FACTS AND THE STEAMROLLER

## The Thin Line Between Persistence and Annoyance

Steamrollers find facts by going straight to their sources – the people with the credentials. Remember, Steamrollers respect anyone with experience, knowledge or education; therefore, successful results and truths come from those with these values. In a fact-finding mission, Steamrollers are not concerned with a person's hierarchy within the company – in fact, they will ask the more senior people in organizations more questions, expecting that they will know more! Steamrollers won't waste their time talking to people who they think don't have the facts.

Steamrollers are very inquisitive and relentless when fact-finding. They are the Nancy Drews and Hardy Boys of the corporate world. This relentlessness is apparent when they begin to "machine gun" questions – rapidly interrogating to get to an understanding. This tactic is seen by most as annoying and intrusive, while the Steamroller considers the exchange as "dialogue" – I ask you a question and you give me an answer! Like the Organizer, they do not accept "yes" or "no" answers, and will continue to ask the same question over and over until they are satisfied.

Steamrollers know when they have enough facts by relying on their gut instincts. When they feel that there's nothing left to ask, learn or understand, they believe they have all the facts and are done. Fact-finding is like a strategy game – sometimes they have to walk away from the situation, think about it and come back with maybe a few more questions. But most of the time, their instincts tell the Steamroller they have all the facts. Interestingly enough, Steamrollers don't need the whole story. As long as they have facts that support their suspicions – you know, four out of five points – they are good to go! Yet Steamrollers know that this also is their blind spot, so if they think there could be an issue with a missing fact, they will go back and ask more questions.

As we have seen, Steamrollers don't get rattled easily, which is why they don't mind receiving misinformation in the eleventh hour. As long as the misinformation was an honest mistake and caught before a solution was implemented, all is workable. When Steamrollers realize they have received incorrect facts before they take action, the situation can easily be fixed. As long as the source is upfront with Steamrollers, the fix might not be pleasant or filled with love, but the action can be salvaged.

But, when Steamrollers realize that they received bad or incorrect facts after the solution has been implemented, they

*The Nanny Cheat Sheet:* **Facts and the Steamroller**

| **How a Steamroller collects facts:** | **How a Steamroller Finds the Facts: Who does s/he depend on?** | **Wrong facts and the Steamroller:** |
|---|---|---|
| As a puzzle s/he is trying to solve. | Going to the source – to the ones who have the credentials, education and knowledge. | S/he likes to get the facts right the first time. |

become upset, because it may be harder to fix – if they can fix it at all!  If they discover that the misinformation was given deliberately – stand back!  Steamrollers will go to the ends of the earth to berate the offending source, letting them know they risked putting themselves, their co-workers and the organization in jeopardy.

*A Nanny Challenge*

Read the story of Josh and Gail, then close the book and see if you can determine where they went wrong.  How did the way different Playground Personalities handle the facts affect the way they handled the problem?  When you have an answer, come back to the book to confirm your thoughts.

## The Story:  Rushing the Gate

Josh, the president of a large distribution firm, believed that six months was plenty of time to design, test and implement a new Accounts Payable System.  During the process, he received weekly progress reports from Gail, the VP of Information Technology.  Frustrated with the timeline, and realizing that every day the project was delayed cost the company a great deal of money, he wanted to "flip the switch" to start using the system.

Gail had invested almost a year of time and management to ensure the system conversion would be successful.  She spent hundreds of hours with her staff designing the system, writing up the project plans and creating training modules so that anyone working with the new system would feel competent.  She believed she was on a proper timeline which had been agreed upon by the company's leadership team.

On a Thursday afternoon, Josh called Gail into a meeting and told her, "Wrap up whatever leftover systems issues you are dealing with, and begin using the system on Monday!" She tried to explain that while the system had been tested repeatedly, she did not want to begin using it until they had 100 percent confidence in the conversion. After all, it affected how company checks would be signed, how bills would be paid and how staff would interact with a new process. Josh wasn't interested in Gail's concerns and just wanted to "roll out" the new multi-million dollar financial system – on Monday!

In spite of her advice and protestations, Gail listened to her boss and "flipped the switch" the following Monday morning. Of course, there were huge system glitches – duplicate checks were cut to some vendors, other vendors didn't get paid at all and some checks were sent out unsigned. When Gail reported this news to Josh, he replied, "What were you doing all this time during the "testing phase?"

## Results: Rushing The Gate

What are the facts in this story? System conversions are always sensitive. Many of those who are not "technology-savvy" do not have an appreciation for what it takes to engineer a successful system conversion. Turning one system off and another on is not as easy as "flipping a switch."

In this scenario, Josh is our Organizer. He had his facts and was frustrated by others' lack of urgency to use the system. Gail, the Steamroller, wanted to make sure the new system was 100 percent ready so her work wasn't labeled a "failure." Managers who don't listen to the "company experts" or who don't want to face facts when it comes to system implementations often find themselves back-peddling when things don't go well.

# CHAPTER SEVEN

# Finding Humor

## A Little Levity Gives Perspective

On a warm summer's evening, I was helping my friend, Annie, at a BBQ party. A group of my girlfriends were gabbing away in the kitchen when Annie's husband, Scott, peeked into the window from the deck to ask for a glass of water.

"With or without ice?" I asked. He looked at me quizzically and, without missing a beat, shouted, "Fire!" To this day, we all laugh when we remember that moment.

Another famous Nanny said it best: "In every job that must be done, there is an element of fun. Find the fun, and SNAP! The job's a game!" Miss Poppins might have been singing to kids, but the essence is the same. Whether your cookout has taken a turn for the worse, or an email has caused panic or discomfort in the workplace, many of life's situations are difficult. Finding humor in these scenarios is critical to being able to effectively evaluate and remedy the situation.

Before we explore this some more, I think I need to explain what I mean by humor. I am not talking about joke telling or speaking comically about a co-worker. Instead, humor is the nugget of information that exposes the absurdity of the situation. This might sound easy, but it is a tricky skill to sharpen. There's a fine – and critically important – line between finding humor in a situation and laughing at a person.

### Humor is Never Personal

Sometimes it's difficult to make the distinction between

laughing at the situation and laughing at the person. Let me end the discussion here: in the workplace, it is always inappropriate to laugh at a co-worker. Period.

When watching viral YouTube.com videos or "America's Funniest Home Videos," it's the situations that are funny – not the people. In a recent video I saw (and like you, I receive dozens of emails every day with links to these videos), a young man fell flat on his face while chasing his cat. The situation was funny. He was not.

A while ago, my girlfriend, a Peacemaker, had a serious operation (she's doing fine, now – no worries). When she went for a follow-up visit, she found herself waiting for over two hours to see the doctor. Needless to say, by the time her name was called, she was thoroughly frustrated and agitated. When she sat on the examining table, her doctor noticed that she was upset.

He pointed toward the window and said, "Charlotte, look out the window at the construction site for that four-tiered garage. When you got here, it was only a hole in the ground!" First, the doctor knew enough to address the situation. Secondly, he chose to see the humor in the situation rather than making an apology. His tactic worked, and the situation was diffused.

## Humor as a Stress Reducer

In most corporate cultures, humor is not a standard practice, and may be seen as out of the ordinary. It's not likely that a company president will bound into the office one day and recommend, "We need to have more humor around here!" However, humor can be found in every department – and is usually a reflection of the manager's demeanor. When the manager makes light of a situation, it sets the tone for how the staff will react – usually with a lighter approach to stress. Conversely, if the manager is intense or serious, the staff will take on that demeanor – which makes for a long day.

I'm not advocating making light of serious situations that affect people's lives, such as accidents or illnesses – but instead, try to "lighten up" when dealing with day-to-day situations that don't necessary go as planned.

When I worked at a large corporation (which shall remain nameless!) our sister company was having issues with inaccurate employee data. Fearing a systemwide problem, our corporate lawyer in Connecticut called me – on a Friday, of course – and said frantically, "You have to pull all the employee files, make copies of their offer letters and send them to Connecticut by Monday." Well, finding the humor in this request wasn't hard – it was flat out absurd! We had over 1,000 files in a bank of file cabinets.

First, I put on my Revolutionary hat. A few ideas flashed in my head, and I sprung into action, knowing that my staff wasn't going to be happy about this emergency assignment. Then, putting on my Organizer hat, I called a meeting with the staff in hopes that we could figure out a team plan to create a checklist and schedule to accomplish the task on time. While I was gathering the team together, Tom (an Organizer, turned Revolutionary in this instance) yelled, "I have an idea!" and bolted out of the room.

As the rest of us stayed focused on our brainstorming, the next thing I knew, Tom flew into the office pushing a copy machine he commandeered from the company library.

"Now we don't have to go far to make the copies!" he exclaimed. We all laughed. This was definitely the stress reliever we all needed – and put us on the road to successfully completing the task on time.

The goal of humor is to relieve stress. Humor relaxes people and puts them at ease. As the manager, humor helps you put things into perspective for the staff and allows the staff to "go with the chaos." If your team implodes due to stress, it takes a great deal of energy to pull everyone back together – and depending upon the level of stress, your team may never fully recover.

When a team never recovers, the staff is likely to "check out" and not actively engage in the work – which will ultimately lead to unresolved conflicts between staff members. It's your job as the manager to make sure people see the lighter side of their work life while taking care of business.

## Humor is Infectious

As businesses grow, divisions and departments become highly interdependent and rely on each other to get their work done. This creates stress as the Software Department depends on IT to make sure the hardware can support the software that they create; the Sales Department depends on the Software Department to have the products ready so the sales force can sell; the Finance Department needs to budget funds to each department so everyone knows how much money they have to spend, etc. You can see how this might lead to a gigantic stress monster that grows as it feeds on the negative energy of discontented staff – and how humor can slay the beast before it has time to destroy.

A start-up software company called me in to evaluate the increasing tension between two of their departments. The company was under a lot of pressure to create products and get them to market. But, there was always tension between IT and Software – IT never had enough storage space for the newly-created data and software never told IT about their development plans, so storage capacity was never ordered accurately.

After conferring, we decided that a fresh, young company needed a fresh, new approach. Each employee was outfitted with

Nerf guns and beanie hats with propellers on top – and together, each department created its own fight song. On Monday morning, the IT and Software departments battled. As the fight songs blared over the PA system, grown-up men and women worked off their tension and stress by confronting each other in a playful way. What was thought to be a game between two departments turned into a company spectator event as people from other departments came to the battle to cheer on the participants. From that day forward, every time an issue arose between the IT and Software departments, the staff remembered their time on the battlefield and worked out their differences in a professional manner.

## Humor and the Playground Personalities

As you can imagine, each Playground Personality has its own take on humor and how it's used in organizations. However, they all share two common elements – not everything is funny to all people and being able to see the absurdity in situations. Each addresses the absurdity in a completely different manner, which is what makes this all the more challenging – and fun.

## HUMOR AND THE PEACEMAKER

Peacemakers set the tone for humor in their department. They are keenly aware that not everyone will participate in the humor – some people may be able to laugh along, while others may not. Because of this, their primary goal is to keep the humor focused on situations and not on people. Peacemakers describe humor as walking a tightrope between people and situations. Balance is crucial so that nothing is misread and no one is offended.

Peacemakers approach situations in a holistic way. To view a situation without seeing the people involved does not give them the whole picture. They look for clues as to why something went wrong, and not who was at fault. This is one of the main differences between Peacemakers and the other Playground Personalities. Maybe we all have something to learn from the Peacemakers!

Peacemakers know that there is great value in stepping back and locating the humor in situations if it is done with dignity and respect. Doing so may bring people closer together and connect them so they feel as though they belong to something larger. Peacemakers use humor to lessen the severity of a situation, so that it allows others to step back and see a different view.

As you are aware, Peacemakers have no intention of hurting anyone's feelings under any circumstance, and they certainly

---

*The Nanny Cheat Sheet:* **Humor and the Peacemaker**

| How a Peacemaker defines humor: | How a Peacemaker uses humor: | Why a Peacemaker values stepping back to see humor in situations: |
|---|---|---|
| Keeps the focus on the situation and how the people are affected. | Being respectful – looking at the situation. | To bring people closer together. |

aren't going to use humor in an inappropriate manner. However, sometimes people misinterpret words and actions, creating hurt feelings. When this happens, Peacemakers jump into action to try and correct the wrong as quickly as possible. They will apologize, but not "fan the flames" to start another incident. If Peacemakers misinterpret the humor, as the manager, they need to really take a look at the situation and what the person took offense to in order to make a good faith effort to address the situation. In either scenario, Peacemakers are naturally believable and will continue to focus on the situation and not the person.

## HUMOR AND THE ORGANIZER

Organizers define humor as seeing a situation for what it really is. Organizers know that being authentic – not blowing off incidents and not being overly serious – help when trying to find the humor in a potentially difficult situation. They are great at diffusing stress by poking fun at themselves and acknowledging their own limitations – a tactic which usually allows others to see the forest through the trees. Organizers challenge people to find the humor in situations and do not allow them to get to the "sky is falling" state of panic.

Organizers know that people do not perform at their highest level of productivity when the environment is stressful and harried. So, while it's important for Organizers to get things done and checked off their lists, they aren't going to sacrifice their team's morale in the process.

Sometimes it's hard for Organizers to separate people from situations – a fault they will admit to freely. Remember, Organizers think of the process first and people second. While their initial urge may be to "choke someone" when things don't go right, they realize that we all make mistakes, and will quickly try to find the humor in the situation by answering the question, "Was the situation fatal or just a nuisance?" Realizing that the matter is not life or death, they put things back into perspective, find the humor in the situation, deal with it and move on.

Many Organizers are serious by nature and must work diligently at not taking things too seriously. They look at things in a linear fashion and have to make a conscious effort to "lighten up" when things are difficult. Also, Organizers have to be careful not to use "gallows humor" – usually an offhanded comment about impending and unavoidable catastrophe in which they are involved.

*The Nanny Cheat Sheet:* **Humor and the Organizer**

| How an Organizer defines humor: | How an Organizer uses humor: | Why an Organizer values stepping back to see humor in situations: |
|---|---|---|
| Seeing things for what they are. | To reduce stress in situations. | To increase productivity and performance in his/her teams. |

In the end, they have to make sure the situation is addressed and finished. Organizers believe that if they are authentic and use humor appropriately, it engenders trust and respect. They know that what was accomplished makes all the difference – and if humor helps to get the job done – they are all for it!

## HUMOR AND THE REVOLUTIONARY

Humor comes naturally to Revolutionaries – and they use this ability to put people at ease from the start. Have you ever connected with someone immediately, feeling as though you have always known them? That person was probably a Revolutionary!

Revolutionaries define humor as a state of being – a device to get through life and see difficult things and relationships more clearly. They evaluate each situation on a case-by-case basis, going out of their way to not place blame or make fun of people, but try to focus on the situation at hand. Treating each scenario as unique is what separates the Revolutionary from other Playground Personalities.

Revolutionaries use humor as an ice-breaker – a funny or light-hearted statement to get the conversation rolling. They are too scattered to remember traditional jokes, so they make poor joke tellers. However, their creativity and natural ease make them incredibly effective and engrossing storytellers. Finding the absurdity in the situation, they are able to pinpoint the humor, laugh at it and translate it to others so they can see it, too.

Stepping back and finding the humor helps Revolutionaries keep their sanity. They dislike coming to work in an environment that has no use for humor. And, while they can deal with situational problems, they really like to deal with people

– especially those who can also chuckle at the absurdity of it all. Revolutionaries gravitate towards people who share this sense of humor – it makes their day go by faster!

Because it's so natural for Revolutionaries to see the humor in life, they are very playful. Their idea of "goofing around" or throwing out innocuous comments – such as "What am I paying you for?" – are often misinterpreted by others. While most coworkers take it with a grain of salt, sometimes people's feelings do get hurt. When this happens, Revolutionaries react with respect to clear any confusion – and file away in their heads the people who cannot handle their type of humor.

*The Nanny Cheat Sheet:* **Humor and the Revolutionary**

| How a Revolutionary defines humor: | How a Revolutionary uses humor: | Why a Revolutionary values stepping back to see humor in situations: |
| --- | --- | --- |
| It's a state of being. | To get through life when handling difficult situations – this may include people. | It keeps him/ her grounded. |

## HUMOR AND THE STEAMROLLER

In typical Steamroller fashion, they usually like to manage complex problems, with many moving parts, all while juggling a million other things – in their opinion, that's comical in itself! But this self-effacing humor is not readily apparent to them.

Remember that Steamrollers are very concerned with their reputations. Any blemish – even one that is light hearted – is to be avoided at any cost. So, while some may find a situation humorous, Steamrollers are often unable to come to the same conclusion. Since they are very serious in whatever they do, when an absurd situation arises, they are probably too involved in it to find the humor in the situation – at least right away. When an absurd situation happens to someone else, though, Steamrollers see the humor much more clearly!

For Steamrollers, the timing of the humor is incredibly important. They believe that humor does help in tense moments – especially if people are working together to accomplish a task. If Steamrollers believe that humor can help or even fix a situation, they will use it because they know it's good for group morale. Steamrollers know that stepping back to see the humor in a situation allows everyone to put things into perspective and see what's ahead. If they're in the middle of a task and bullets start to fly – as long as they can sit back and see that progress is being made – Steamrollers can find the humor.

Steamrollers know if you cannot find the humor when under pressure, people will collapse. We know that during times of change and uncertainty, Steamrollers work at their best. They brainstorm multiple possibilities, put documents together and try to draw conclusions – all in the face of the unknown. And, while they are fine working under these conditions, they realize that their staff may not be. So, when their staff gets weary, they bring in the toys – punching bags, dartboards and basketball hoops – all to give people a much-needed break.

When team building, Steamrollers know that if everyone can laugh with each other, they will take risks because they are in it together. They instinctively know that when a new person is brought into a team, the best strategy is for the current staff to "hold their tongues." In this way, trust and respect can be rebuilt, and all can move forward.

*One big caveat:* Steamrollers sometimes do not separate the situation from the people involved. In their mind, it's the people who make a situation funny. Because of this, Steamrollers want their staff to have "thick skin" – which, if you've ever worked for one, you already know is necessary to keep your own sanity.

---

*The Nanny Cheat Sheet:* **Humor and the Steamroller**

| How a Steamroller defines humor: | How a Steamroller uses humor: | Why a Steamroller values stepping back to see humor in situations: |
|---|---|---|
| It's about personal reputation. | To suspend tense moments. | To put things back into perspective. |

*A Few Nanny Challenges*

Time for two more stories. After reading each, close the book and think about what Playground Personality each character is, and what is the humor in the situation. When you open the book, flip back to this page and we can compare notes.

## The Story: Who Let the Bugs Out?

I took a consulting gig at a small biotech firm that was trying to find out why their beehives were collapsing. It took a little time for me to become comfortable in a facility in which two rooms over a swarm of bees was being bred, fed and living their lives flying around in large mesh cages.

One afternoon, while training some new managers, a red light on the wall began to flash. I figured this couldn't be a good sign. From the window in the door, I could see a few people in lab coats rushing down the hall in the direction of the bees! Needless to say, I stayed put. The show must go on, so I continued with the managers at the table, while all the while people in the halls scurried about and the light continued pulsing, casting a disturbing red glow on everyone's face. About 10 minutes later, the light stopped blinking, and a Senior VP walked into the conference room. He explained that a breach in protocol had been made and a small container of bees had been dropped during transfer from one lab to the next. A few had escaped and were flying freely about the laboratory. We were reassured they were now contained, and that no one was at risk.

He left the room to a stunned silence. After a brief moment, I collected myself, straightened out my skirt, grabbed the laser pointer and kept on going.

## Results:  Who Let the Bugs Out?

With an unflinching charm, I kept my cool – even while facing angry bees!  I Steamrolled through the training session.  If
I had been in my Revolutionary mode, I probably would have
joined the fight (especially if it had involved puppies instead of
insects).  As a Peacemaker, I would probably have been more
apologetic to the managers at the table.  And as an Organizer, I
would have taken notes about what was going on to question the
Senior VP at a later time.

So what was funny?  The absurd situation – escaped bees,
frantic scientists and red lights – seems like a scene from a screw-
ball comedy.  Keeping my cool and continuing with the training
added a touch of flair to the proceedings – like icing on the cake.

## The Story:  The Firing That Never Was

I assisted a medium-sized company with a plan to reduce
their workforce.  Yes, I was the one who had to lay off people.
Part of the plan was to delete a user's access to the company's
computer system and email while they were in conference with
the HR Department, learning of their fate.  A list of those accounts to be deactivated was created, and only the head of the
department and the IT Technician were given copies.

Bettye, the department head, noticed that an email to her
staffer, Michael, had bounced back to her as undeliverable.  Even
with Michael out of the office at a client site, this should not
have happened.  She called down to IT to speak with Ravi, the IT
Technician.  "Ravi, why is email bouncing back from Michael's
email?" she questioned.  He responded that he had disabled
access per the plan – after all, his name was on the list.  Panicked
– after all, she didn't remember seeing Michael's name on the list

– Bettye looked at her list.

"I think I see the problem. You deleted Michael K. Instead, you should have deleted Michael R.," she discovered. Seeing how this mistake could easily be made, they both laughed – and immediately reactivated the account. When Michael returned to the office, he had no inkling the he had been "fired" and "rehired" while away.

## Results: The Firing That Never Was

It's sad when an organization needs to let people go. It is a stressful time for everyone, and even with the most careful planning things go wrong.

In this story, Bettye was working in a Peacemaker mode, trying to fix the problem quickly and without notice from anyone else. Ravi, the Organizer, did as told – deactivate those on the list in the order as required.

This comedy of mistaken identity (and not reading the memo more clearly) was probably not so funny when first told to Michael. However, with time, it is incidents like these that we all can look back on and laugh.

# CHAPTER EIGHT

# Tact

**The Art of Making it Happen!**

I can hear you muttering, "So what? But how is all of this going to matter when I am actually working with my staff?"

We've spent the time together learning about self-awareness and how it's the key to understanding others; we walked through the importance of facing facts, being respectful and using humor appropriately – all of which should contribute to your being a happy and productive manager.

While the first four points of Neglected Knowledge are our "parts," the fifth, using tact, is where the rubber meets the road – where you put it all together!

Remember that at the end of the day, you are paid for getting things done. In your case as a new manager, getting those "things" done is very different from working through others, or even working by yourself.

## Finesse The Flock

Anyone can implement a plan. Following the directions on the package of oatmeal takes only a few steps so that almost anyone – even a child – can do it. Tact is the ability to implement a plan with style – caring, attention to detail, consideration of staff and ability to steer to another course if needed. Adding a pinch of cinnamon to your oatmeal is just the extra "flair" that turns an ordinary meal into an exceptional experience.

Tact is realized by three simple actions: creating a plan, getting the buy-in from your team to move forward and implementing the plan in a way that gets the most out of your effort and your team's efforts – all to benefit the organization and its people. It's no surprise that each Playground Personality reacts differently to how you will use tact – and, I will walk you step-by-step through each personality and how to put it all together.

You know there is a wide spectrum of people in your office – those who make things happen, those who wait for things to happen and those who say, "What the hell happened?" I am sure you have come across many of these folks throughout your career. Developing your own management style through the use of tact will help you cut through these differences – and get things done. People want to be involved in decisions and plans that affect their work. Getting your staff involved from the start will bring them together – but more importantly, will provide credibility. Your staff wants to work for someone who is approachable and takes the time to figure out what brings out the best in them.

## Think Before You Speak, Write or Act

Doesn't that sound like something a Nanny would jab at you umpteen times a day? I think most of us strive to do the right thing most of the time. In a busy workplace, often it is so hectic that you can't think before you respond or speak. There are always tensions that could cause us to snap – after all, we're human! However, as the one in charge, you must always be aware that no one wants to work with a manager who could "flip out" at any point in time. It makes for a jittery team.

In the heat of the moment, it's easy to blurt out the first thing that comes to mind – which is usually insulting. This is instinctual, and most people don't even realize they're doing it. Offending your staff will only cause other issues – so THINK before you speak, write or act.

As a Steamroller, my hotheadedness can go from 0 to 10 in about a nanosecond – so I have to keep it in check at all times! When I first catch myself about to instinctually react – I **STOP**, close my eyes for a few moments and count to 10. Believe it or not, this small pause can help you collect your thoughts so the next words from your mouth are insightful and not insulting.

## Recollections of Past Managers

I was brought into a large corporation for a leadership retreat. Many of the new senior management team had been on the job for less than a year – and were overwhelmed by their positions. The Corporate Nanny to the rescue!

On the first day, I conducted an exercise to open the dialogue for the rest of the week. I asked the participants to reflect on managers they have worked for throughout their lifetimes – and write down what made each one "good" or "not-so-good."

When the groups began to debrief their flipcharts, a pattern quickly emerged. It didn't matter what type of manager they were talking about, what type of company they worked for or what level of management was discussed – their responses fell into three distinct categories: interpersonal skills, intelligence and technical competency.

While everyone agreed that it's important for managers to be competent and smart in their fields or trades, most of the feedback fell into the interpersonal category. I know it would be difficult to be a Squad Leader of a Special Victims Unit (SVU) if you were never an officer on the street. Obviously, you need a certain level of technical competency to lead your squad. But without good interpersonal skills – even with a high level of competency – your effectiveness would be compromised.

Almost 80 percent of all the comments were descriptions

about interpersonal skills.  They read something like this:

| **"Good" Managers** | **"Not-so-Good" Managers** |
| --- | --- |
| • Listen well | • Aloof or nasty |
| • Genuinely care | • Poor communicators |
| • Respectful | • Know it all |
| • Take time to understand | • Not responsive |
| • Explain the "big picture" | • Tell, do not ask |

Group after group confirmed that their lists agreed with almost everyone else's.  The groups were serious about their reflections, and it became apparent that the interpersonal issues were universal.  At the end of the debriefing, one manager uttered to another manager, "Wow, I hope I never did any of those things!"

For the SVU Leader mentioned above, it's not just about the time on the street.  Good managers have a passion for people, the ability to get people to work together and make people think and feel that the work they do is tremendously important to the greater good.

## Step 1:  Let's Make a Plan!

As basic as this sounds, you'd be surprised how many people embark on projects without a plan.  Here's the main point:  if you are working in a team or if you are managing a team – it's everyone's responsibility to help create the plan – not just the manager's.

I remember working with a senior team about re-engineering the way their Marketing Department functioned when a team member chimed in, "I'll do whatever you what me to do – just tell me the plan."  From experience, I knew this was going to be a harder job than I thought!

When the team looks to the manager for answers and solutions, the wheels will fall off the wagon before it gets out of the barn. If it were that easy, why would managers even need teams? They should be able to run things by themselves, right? Wrong! It's the people who help create the plan, and it's the same people who create success – or failure.

I have a simple Nanny Tip to help me create plans. The sound of a big sigh of relief is *"Wwwwwh!"* – the same acronym for the steps to devise a successful plan:

1. **WHY** *are we embarking on the project?* Categorize what's new, different, broken or needs improvement. Be clear on what we are trying to make better, fix or solve.

2. **WHAT** *are the moveable parts?* Identify all the pieces of the puzzle that need to be addressed.

3. **WHO** *is responsible for making the parts work?* Assign everyone a role and responsibility as it relates to the project. Figure out if you have the right mix of talent.

4. **WHERE** *is the impact expected to be recognized?* Know what part or parts of the organization (entire company, specific function or department) you are trying to address.

5. **WHEN** *does it have to happen?* Recognize deadlines.

6. **HOW** *is it going to work?* Be familiar with what happens when the systems get turned on.

Most of the bases are covered when you have the answers to these questions. However, as you answer these points, additional questions will begin to surface. These additional questions are just as important, so do not forget to address them, also.

As you ask these questions, you will probably realize that you do not have all of the answers on hand. Don't panic – many of these will come to light as the project continues. Having a framework that keeps you focused, though, is critical for success. Refer back to Chapter 6 on Facing Facts and remember the Playground Personalities. This will prevent you from stumbling into any pitfalls when collecting the facts.

So how detailed does the plan have to be? That depends on the magnitude of the project and the Playground Personalities involved. Remember, all Playground Personalities agree that a plan is essential when managing change – it's how the intricacy of the plan unfolds that varies between them. Some want a "locked down" strategy and need every "nook and cranny" covered, while others only want a loose framework to work through as the situation develops and changes.

Developing a plan means knowing the vision, the resources, how the roles and responsibilities will be divided up and communicating to the staff as frequently as possible. Obviously, you can't do this without having solid working relationships with your staff and others, both inside and outside the organization. Refer back to Chapter 5 on Respect to refresh your memory on what motivates people to help – and what shuts them down. Respecting others helps to build a solid platform for your plan to work successfully. Without having all of the facts and garnering the appropriate respect – all wrapped up in a carefully thought out plan – you will never get the buy-in needed to make it happen.

## Step 2: Let's Get the Buy-in!

Planning is easy. Getting everyone on board is not so simple. Emailing your friends about dinner at Chez Françoise at 8:00 p.m. is easy. Getting everyone there on time is often like corralling cats.

You may have the best plan in the world, but if no one is there to help implement it – what good is it? Getting the buy-in is done through clear and well-timed communications. Typically, there are three times when getting the buy-in is easiest: one, at the beginning of the process when people are excited about something new or about change in general; two, in the middle before things are finalized – especially if something might be off track and another course of action is needed; and three, at the end when the process is complete and your staff must be trained on the new procedures as a result of the plan. Missing any of these opportunities makes it much harder to get the buy-in – that is if you'll ever get it at all.

### Communicate Clearly

When you are able to get everyone on board pretty easily, call yourself blessed, as these cases are few and far between. But most of the time, getting the buy-in will take some effort. Make no mistake – getting buy-in is hard work – but it is totally worth it! During these times, you cannot communicate enough with your staff and the organization. People need to hear about the status of the plan, and, when possible, they like to be asked their opinion on how to steer it toward success. This dialogue needs to be a two-way street – listen closely, and you will hear the real issues that might be railroading your efforts. When staff is not updated, they might work on assumptions, rumors and even "made up" information! You know this will only lead to failure. I remember an old TV show in which a character said to, "… never assume. It makes an 'ass' out of 'u' and 'me!'"

When going through a rough spot in the implementation of a plan, the last thing a manager needs is to have the team be unaware of the goals. Keep the lines of communication open. I know that there are times when all of the details cannot be shared openly or in a timeframe that is opportune. Sometimes, there are details that cannot be shared due to legalities or privacy concerns. That's fine – just communicate what you know to date. Continue to communicate the message as frequently as possible to relieve the stress of the entire organization. Whatever you do, as the manager, if you do not know the answer to a question, do not make one up! Write down the question, research the answer and get back to your staff with accurate and appropriate information.

I gave some free advice to a Steamroller friend of mine who thought he was over-communicating. He likes to send his staff daily emails of what is yet to be completed and what goals lie ahead. I explained to him that it was not the number of emails, but the tone that was causing his staff to ignore them. Using tact – figuring out your management style – will go a long way to help avoid this concern. When he finally changed the email format from bullet points and lists to short paragraphs discussing the ramifications of each goal, he was seen as less of a microman-ager and more approachable.

## Step 3:  Making It Happen

There's a reason why Native Americans, the Scots in "Brave-heart" and NFL players paint their faces – when going into battle, it is important to show your strength.

Now, your workplace is not a battlefield (I hope), but putting on your "game face" is very important when addressing your staff. It's the role of the manager to be a rock during times of uncertainty. Be calm and in control when communicating face-to-face – you can't looked alarmed, scared or frustrated. Exude confidence – think Clint Eastwood in any of the "Dirty Harry" movies or Sigourney Weaver in the "Aliens" trilogy.

Nervous laughter can be distracting and a giveaway as to your true emotional state. And whatever you do, never blame anyone in public – tearing someone down will cause you a loss of respect you will never be able to overcome – no matter who the Playground Personalities are. Stick to the facts when communicating and practice your talking points before you deliver them live. Another good example of thinking before you speak.

## Be Flexible

You will encounter roadblocks – people who opt-out of the plan; those who won't buy-in to begin with; systems that won't work as planned; regulations, policies or bureaucracies that are unflinching and confining – all seeming to plot against you.

Whatever happens – remain flexible – a concept that is often difficult for some Playground Personalities to embrace. While sticking to the plan in spite of the consequences is a bad idea, changing plans every few days also will work against you. Both of these strategies will cause you to lose people – and their respect – along the way. Staying the course when things aren't going well tells others that you are not willing to hear their feedback. Altering the plans before they solidify can cause stress when the team starts to think they are heading down the right road, only to take a sharp turn down an unknown and uncharted path.

After all of my years working with companies of every size

and people at every level, I firmly believe that it is better to steer your ship into potentially murky waters than to head back to port and start over again. I know this might go against what you have learned before – many of you have been taught to cut your losses and try again.

Just as implementing the plan must be done with careful timing, so must alterations. Make a change too early, and you might miss an opportunity; changing course too late may cause resentments that can be difficult to recover from. I know this sounds tricky – and it is. Just remember: if you do nothing at all, your inaction will destroy everything.

Changing a portion of the plan does not mean that it was a failure. However, not recognizing that some aspect of the plan needs a tweak is a failure. If you communicate openly, encourage your staff to give feedback on the course set and seriously re-evaluate the facts, you can move forward toward clearer skies.

## TACT AND THE PLAYGROUND PERSONALITIES

Not surprisingly, each of the Playground Personalities has its own twist on tact. Remember, there is no right or wrong way to enact a plan – just the way you choose to act to maximize the results and performance of your team. You may have to call upon a few of the Personalities in order to get the whole plan completed. Not only is that okay, it's encouraged! Knowing your staff and how they react to change, communication and your management style will make for a smoother ride to success.

This chapter is significantly different from the previous ones. In them, I described how each of the Playground Personalities react to fact-finding, respect or humor and how to determine a person's primary personality. This chapter is about *YOU* – how you, based on your Playground Personality, should approach planning and tactful implementation of the strategy.

Each section might sound like a psychic prediction – and in a way it is. Your Playground Personality does determine how you act and I am sure you will see how it has formed your actions in the past. However, don't be afraid to act in another Personality if the situation arises. Let this be a guide to help you go forward.

# So, You Are a Peacemaker.

As a Peacemaker, you like to have a plan. However, the details of the plan depend on the projects you're working on and whether or not you're starting from scratch or managing a project that's already on course. You work with your staff and others to outline the vision that has been established (perhaps by someone else) and make sure everyone knows what the end result should be. You do a good job ensuring all of your staff are on the same page and their goals are aligned with those of the vision.

Peacemakers do not create a project plan after one meeting. The development of a plan takes time and the consideration of others. You plug each staff members' name in a spreadsheet – not for your own edification, but to make sure that the right staff is working on the plan. You sift through all of the available information by throwing out a wide net, and culling through to get to the bits that are critical for your staff to perform well. As the manager, you want to make sure that everyone's roles and responsibilities are clearly defined, and that people are comfortable with their work expectations.

It's not surprising that for Peacemakers, the most important resource is people. You spend a great deal of time taking an inventory of your staff: Who is your best researcher, systems guru, negotiator, etc.? Does that person have the talent and skills?

Are they interested in the plan? Are they available to help? Do they have the time and capacity to do the work? Once people are identified and brought into the plan, you are ready to address additional resources.

Institutional knowledge and wisdom gained through the process are very important to the Peacemaker. You will use any sources of information – inside and outside the company – to help develop and steer the plan. The past is used as a reference point to understand what might not have worked before, which helps to guide the new plan moving forward. Money issues are not a concern for the day-to-day implementation of the plan. If you do not have the answer to a question, and there is no information in the resources, you are able to make educated assumptions and make assignments accordingly to begin the work. You develop your plans by looking at the big picture first, then tearing it down to simpler terms – it's easiest to work in smaller pieces. The Peacemaker's philosophy is "if you don't know where you are going, any road will get you there!" So you define where you are going and then plan the road you'll take.

Peacemakers value discussions to determine mid-course corrections. You bring everyone on the team together to talk about what is working and identify the obstacles. When you hear, "Oh, that didn't work," you take the time to debrief the staff and learn what insights can be gained. You're interested in knowing what the team has learned from the very first obstacles.

While Peacemakers are open to hearing about challenges, they are not willing to listen to staff members placing blame on one another or a staff member's anger. You know that some team members may have to be replaced in order to keep the ship on course. If the mid-course correction involves an outside vendor who isn't delivering on promises, that vendor will be removed and a new vendor brought in to complete the plan.

Peacemakers do not like surprises, which is why they provide ample opportunities for status reports and staff updates. You don't want to wait to the end to find out the project is over budget!

Peacemakers always try to get the staff to buy in from the start, since working in a vacuum is never desirable. Early in the game, you identify the players and what tasks should go to each based on their skills. In an attempt to get as much buy-in as possible, you may even gather additional resources from around the organization – perhaps asking senior leaders to help with staff communication to show their support. Once you know who the players are, you are very good at getting them immediately involved in the process. You may call a special meeting or conduct a focus group to obtain feedback. Doing so allows you to share the goals with your staff, engage the staff in the plan moving forward and help them see how their input affects the future. If necessary, you are open to bringing in an outside facilitator to bring out the best in your staff. Everything you do is in the spirit of building relationships and giving staff the time to settle in to a new way of doing things.

***The upside of the Peacemaker and Planning:*** Working collaboratively helps make people feel good about the plan. You are incredibly good at facilitating small group discussions and getting many different points of view on the table so people believe they are heard. You can see the big picture and excel at delegating tasks, trusting people to carry out their responsibilities. You think creatively and solve problems with ease. You also are adept at managing conflict and working with people to build relationships. You have patience with both people and processes and are willing to take a little extra time to allow your staff to work through things. When working with your staff, you help instill

*The Nanny Cheat Sheet:* **Tact and the Peacemaker**

| How detailed does your plan have to be? | How should you communicate? |
|---|---|
| Details are important to you, but you don't feel compelled to have a plan right away. | State the plan upfront and allow people the opportunity to provide feedback. |
| **How should you manage mid-course corrections?** | **What should you be aware of?** |
| You should talk with people who are affected by the change to gather more feedback. | You like managing the big picture – it's the details you don't like. |

confidence in what they are doing and help them believe in themselves. You allow people the leeway to let them grow so they can be successful.

**The downside of the Peacemaker and Planning:** You are not good with the nitty-gritty details. This information is too tedious to deal with, so you rely (and trust) others to work through this information, ensuring the plan is on course. You want things to just "happen," or you want to fix problems as they arise and then move on. You have a long fuse, so you do not become frustrated easily. You are keenly aware that you may let issues go on too long without addressing them, which makes for uncomfortable back peddling. It irks you when your staff won't play nice, or when they argue with one another. This behavior is not something you have much patience for.

# So, You Are an Organizer.

As an Organizer, it's not surprising that your plans need to be pretty detailed, so you have a clear path to follow to complete the tasks. While you have to provide the framework for the plan – after all, lists make a great frame from which to hang any plan – you don't necessarily have to be the one to put the plan together. Collaboration with others is one of your strengths – and getting an early buy-in from your staff comes naturally to you.

You prefer to have a master plan, with calls for action under each category. These calls to action are the meat on the bones for your master plan. These might include mapping out the process, assigning responsibilities, knowing you have the right talent for the right work and communicating to all of your staff so they are aware of their roles and responsibilities. However, you are leery of being locked into a plan – you need breathing room for flexibility in case you have to divert resources, such as people or money. Therefore, your plan needs to be broad enough to encompass all of the parameters, but narrow enough so everyone knows what they have to do to successfully complete it.

You need to understand the "what" as it relates to the plan. What needs to be done and what we need to do to get this done. For you, it all boils down to getting things done.

The first thing you probably want – and with good reason – is data; as much as can be gathered. You think that if you have enough data, you can move more quickly to complete the work. You need to get to the people who have the data or the answers to the "what" questions – whether they are inside or outside the organization.

You assign the appropriate responsibility to each Personality's strength. You want your staff in the forefront, not working behind the scenes! It also is very important for you to have people with institutional knowledge together around a table to talk through the different options of the plan while it is forming. And of course, you need to know how the plan is going to be financed. After all, what is the point of creating elaborate schemes if there is no way to fund them?

You need to see the plan on paper so you know it's real. You love charts and spreadsheets that are color-coded and highlighted so you can pick out the hot spots. They have lots of columns – including the most important "To Do" column – complete with a space for a check-off mark! There's a sense of security and peace when you know you have all the "i's" dotted and "t's" crossed – it confirms that there is a plan anyone can see it's a plan, and you believe it will work – even if deep inside you know that something will inevitably not go according to plan!

You don't like finger pointing – you want people to dig in and keep working at it. And for those who need a "kick in the pants," you are willing to give it to them – with care and respect of course! You know it's important to nip any chaos in the bud, because you don't want it to negatively impact the entire organization.

Organizers don't like surprises, but you have figured out a way to manage them. You know your plan could be the best plan ever – even if you did not put in enough flexibility for the inevitable monkey wrench. Here's where humor comes into play – since you don't want people to freak out, you reduce stress and tension by using appropriate humor.

You don't like re-work (and who does?) but you know you must answer the question "Why aren't we getting the results we want?" when the plan's outcomes don't accomplish its goals. You know the outcomes or desired results haven't changed, so you have to change course because what you're doing isn't working!

Organizers can get into a panic mode about planning. So you try to remove the "Oh my gosh" factor by brainstorming and developing alternative ideas. You expect people who are a part of the process to give you feedback on anything and everything: resource issues, misunderstandings, personnel issues. You expect people to tell you straight out, "You aren't going to be able to do it this way and here's why." You want to know what correction is needed, and what you need to do to get back on track.

Getting buy-in from your staff is a very conscious event for Organizers. You relish kick-off meetings, announcing a new era, communicating the overall objectives and goals and preparing people for change. You are smart enough to notice when there's resistance. When you sense this, you call people in for a one-on-one to hear their concerns and try to address them. Yes, getting buy-in is a time monster, and sometimes you think you don't have the time to do it. That's when you call in others to help deliver the message. You know there's a big payoff when getting buy-in is done correctly – so you make the time.

**The upside of the Organizer and Planning:** Time is of the essence when it comes to developing a plan. Optimizing resources – both people and processes – and delivering results is what you are all about. You are very tenacious and will figure out

---

*The Nanny Cheat Sheet:* **Tact and the Organizer**

| **How detailed does your plan have to be?** | **How should you communicate?** |
|---|---|
| Details are important to you. Outline the plan well enough to get to the finish line. | Frequently, clearly and concisely without giving too many details. |
| **How should you manage mid-course corrections?** | **What should you be aware of?** |
| Use humor to set a level playing field and call in the experts! | You manage time well and sometimes get impatient with others who aren't working hard enough. |

---

how to get something done – "do or die." You include others who have had similar experiences to join in and help work on the plan because you value their experiences. You understand the industry they are working in, and know what has and has not worked in the past. You are able to keep multiple balls in the air, and rarely drop any – an incredible feat! Your need to drive for results eases the minds of the organization and the people who are in it – they know they are in good hands!

**The downside of the Organizer and Planning:** Your eye is always on the prize, so you have little patience for those who don't "get it" – especially after you have explained it five times before! You subscribe to the old adage, "If you want something done right, do it yourself." You want everything done yesterday, so you tend to throw delegation out the window and do everything yourself. The clock (the one in your mind) is always ticking, and you're thinking, "If this gets done sooner, we'll be done and we'll have the results." Sometimes your "do or die" strategy drives others away, because no matter how hard your staff is working, you don't think it's ever enough. This is a dangerous pitfall – be careful, and remember the bigger picture.

# So, You Are a Revolutionary.

For Revolutionaries, making plans is almost like being in the Wild West! In many cases, you are asked to work on non-routine or emergency plans – ones that you have experienced before, so you have a pretty good idea of what's involved and how to troubleshoot the situation. You build strategies based on the level of detail involved with the plan. If the situation only needs a quick fix, you will immediately get the appropriate staff involved and begin to hash out the plan right then and there. You like a lot of open dialogue to keep ideas flowing. Only when the situation is critical will you bring in the finer details in creating your plan. You do not use a cookie-cutter approach to anything, let alone when making plans. After all, the real world is very different from what you learned in textbooks.

For Revolutionaries to do their best work, they need four resources: people, equipment, time and money. You approach creating a plan like a partnership – you know the ultimate responsibility is with you, but you cannot do it alone. You are keenly aware of your staff's skills and assign tasks accordingly.

While you like the idea of "the more the merrier," you recognize that you must work with qualified people who have the right backgrounds – the ones who will deliver. All others might be fun to run around with, but will not be good for the success of your plan. You believe in having plenty of back-up staff, so when one person needs to be replaced, it is seamless.

After staff is refined and ready, Revolutionaries head to the white board for brainstorming and idea development. Once ideas are solidified, a clean copy is transferred to a flipchart so you can rip off each sheet and hand it to the person who will be responsible for making that part of the plan happen. Your "To Do's" will end up very differently than that of an Organizer – you are unlikely to check off the completed tasks – if you can even find your list at all after the project starts! You make sure that your staff has enough computer equipment and software, cell phones, 2-way radios, office space – everything they need to get the plan in gear.

Of course, time is of the essence – so you are apt to use it wisely. Finally, while accounting is not your strong suit, you realize that you are responsible for controlling administrative, operational and unexpected expenses – which you do with finesse.

Revolutionaries love to play games and brainstorm, taking each large idea nugget and whittling it away to the central core so that task can be worked on immediately. You challenge people to think of one great idea – one that's going to save everyone time and trouble in the end. Depending on how fast the plan is proceeding, this process can be amazingly quick or take an interminable amount of time. You only need to know the "guts" of the idea and leave the detail planning to the experts. You are perceptive, and if you get the hunch that something is going to go wrong, you will jump in and fix it before chaos starts. You relish thinking through problems before they happen – it keeps you on your toes!

If things are not going according to plan – and in the Revolutionary's world, they rarely do – the phrase "What the hell!" might be heard uttered down the hallway! You are quick to go back to the drawing board and see what might have been missed. You believe that re-working a plan is fine, especially after listening to your staff to brainstorm another angle. Mid-course corrections are expected and accounted for from the start. Plan B was probably developed along with Plan A (though in not as much detail), so when a change in the plan is needed, it's easy to implement. If the whole original plan doesn't work – you stop, rethink it and go to the Plan B to see if it will work. Sometimes you pick pieces from both Plans A & B – because you don't have to start from the beginning. Sometimes you'll take shortcuts through the things that worked and only focus on the things that didn't work. Sometimes the strategies or tactics don't have to change; it's how you apply them that have to change! Anyway, you are confident with your decision, which your staff senses and respects.

Through this change process, Revolutionaries need to communicate openly with their staff to keep the flow of ideas running smoothly. You know you can't prepare for everything that could go wrong – and you actually get a little rush when you realize there was a fact you were missing, since it gives you another challenge to overcome! You thrive in this situation and make adjustments as you go along.

Revolutionaries hate loose ends hanging anywhere, so getting the buy-in up front is vital. You are charming, because you make people part of the process from the beginning and do not impose upon them. You ask for input even if you really don't want it – just to gauge people's thoughts and make sure you aren't missing anything. You allow others to co-own the plan from early in the game, which inspires them to work more closely together. For those who are reluctant to buy-in, you turn on that charisma and

---

*The Nanny Cheat Sheet:* **Tact and the Revolutionary**

| **How detailed does your plan have to be?** | **How should you communicate?** |
|---|---|
| Not very detailed – just enough to get you started. | Include everyone in the plan and the updates – make it real for people! |
| **How should you manage mid-course corrections?** | **What should you be aware of?** |
| With a Coke and a smile! You expect to make changes – so you're always ready! | You aren't afraid to jump in. But, you can tend to explode! |

---

might use a little trick up your sleeve to get them to comply, such as stating, "I understand your point, but if the plan goes belly-up, make no mistake – I own the responsibility." However, your gut lets you know when you're trying too hard – it's an indicator that the person you're wooing is probably not right for the task. Listen to yourself.

**The upside of the Revolutionary and Planning:** Calm under pressure is your motto. You might find yourself getting worked up over the stupid stuff, but when it counts, you always pay attention and are ready to forge ahead. Your staff trusts that you have their backs – and that loyalty goes both ways, which is why you invest the time to get to know them and how they function. People usually follow Revolutionaries from company to company, because you are stand-up men and women who take the heat for your staff – and don't make a big deal about it. You have thick skin. You know where the buck stops and are not afraid to take the responsibility and all that goes along with it. You like to "kick the ball as hard as you can," and respect others on your team who do the same. No job is too big or too small – and no job is above or beneath you. You are direct in your responses and communicate the good, bad and ugly. Because you do not require a lot of structure, you are able to handle the curve balls that will come your way – and actually like it! When everything is running smoothly, you might find yourself a little bored, so you'll try to find another project to get involved in.

***The downside of the Revolutionary and Planning:*** You are the "I told you so" men and women – especially when you tried your hardest to change an aspect of a plan, but were over-ruled. You may get agitated quickly, but this usually lasts only a few seconds. Afterwards, you do not hold grudges or harbor bad feelings. However, when you do "blow up," your staff better run! You get frustrated when people are not moving fast enough, or not pulling their weight. You need your staff to run at 100 mph, but know that you cannot kill them in the process. Although you respect intelligence, people who are too wordy tend to drive you insane – you want them to get to the point like you do!

# So, You Are a Steamroller.

As a Steamroller, your focus is on the overall strategy: the big picture and the objectives that support the vision. You're less concerned about the details of the plan, leaving them to the staff you've surrounded yourself with – the smartest people you can find. You give your staff the latitude to do what has to be done. You are likely to put your vision on paper – but in an abbreviated form, because you know that it will be constantly refined before it becomes final. Refining the plan means jotting down key points you want to address, filling in the blanks as it relates to areas of responsibility and delegating tasks to appropriate staff members. A major concern for you is to have a vision that focuses on how growth strengthens the organization and its people.

Once you've identified the plan, you need resources to ensure its value: people, knowledge and calendars. First, you depend on your people. You have confidence in them to get the work done – after all, you respect them for their credentials and work history. You ask up front if people are up for the task, and provide attainable professional development experiences by assigning tasks that stretch your staff's thinking. You know people can't go from A to D in one huge leap, so you work with your staff to help them learn and grow and walk from A to B to C to D in successful steps.

You rely on calendars to establish mile markers throughout the plan – a starting point, a few check-in points and a finishing point. You know where everyone should be at a certain date, so you build in a constant feedback loop by arranging check-in meetings regularly. Your constant search for feedback, new information and validation of the vision ensure that the plan stays on target.

Lastly, Steamrollers require a body of knowledge to bring credibility to the plan. You refer to organizational documents, charts, historical information, laws, regulations – whatever you can get your hands on – or should I say, whatever your staff can get their hands on. This vast amount of data is analyzed and thought through to confirm or refine your plan.

Steamrollers clarify their vision by going to confidants, close advisors or their immediate management circles. You believe that these respected sources bring momentum to the vision, which will excite the rest of the staff, creating a better chance for success. You develop and modify plans as information comes to light, and know the importance of assigning appropriate staff to the new tasks. You like to bring the plan to others for their input, essentially building the plan on its journey.

Like Organizers, you don't like surprises! Your philosophy is that bad news never gets better with time. Steamrollers are not interested in playing "gotcha" games – if the staff is stuck, you want to know about it for immediate resolution. Because you usually work in a climate where everything has an element of risk to it, you recognize that mid-course corrections are inevitable (and essential). You'll go back to the original core group who you relied on in the beginning of the plan and state, "I don't think this is working and here's why." This conversation usually results in identifying what can be salvaged and if a mid-course correction can even be effective. If it can, you immediately get the staff reconnected and start brainstorming a range of options to move ahead. If it's decided that a mid-course correction will not work, you are okay with scrapping the mission – even if a little disappointed. Steamrollers like to see their plans completed, but there's no policy that requires you to have to finish everything!

It's natural for Steamrollers to get buy-in from people. After all, you depend on the synergies of smart people. You are

---

*The Nanny Cheat Sheet:* **Tact and the Steamroller**

| **How detailed does your plan have to be?** | **How should you communicate?** |
|---|---|
| Details aren't as important as having a vision – the details will come later. | Talk through the big picture and offer up details to the folks who may need some help thinking differently in the future. |
| **How should you manage mid-course corrections?** | **What should you be aware of?** |
| Communicate to people in hopes of gaining their confidence and trust. | You're willing to take risks and get impatient with people who aren't ready for change. |

---

confident with the people working with you, and that makes the process easy. Getting the best out of everyone is what you strive for – doing so makes you look smart and credible, too. You depend on yourself, and not others, to deliver the message and get the staff buy-in. You are skilled at laying out your vision and the direction the organization will take. You enjoy fielding questions and explaining what's up for grabs, and what's not. You believe that people should just "get it," but if they do not, you are willing to spend the time to ensure your staff understands.

**The upside of the Steamroller and Planning:** You have too much pride to fail on a mission, so you will do anything to do it right and succeed. You exude commitment and confidence, and are effective at delivering the message that "we" will succeed! Because of your passion about the work, you're able to rally people around an issue. You're able to create a clear strategy and point of view about the goals of that vision. You're very good at recruiting talent to fill the needs of the plan. You enjoy risk-taking opportunities and aren't afraid of change or hard work.

**The downside of the Steamroller and Planning:** You don't have a lot of patience for people who have difficulty with change. These people rub you the wrong way, and you want to scream, "Come on, this is cool stuff! Can't you just go with the flow? Change is good!" Be careful, and remember to think before you speak (remember counting to 10). You have to "kick the tires" and reflect on the facts before you charge ahead. You know you can drive your staff crazy, especially Organizers and Peacemakers who want all the details upfront. You don't have patience for people who need direction on tasks that require specific knowledge. You're a "big picture" person – it's all about getting there and capturing the details of the journey along the way.

*A Nanny Challenge*

Let's give it a go and put the whole thing together! I challenge you to first figure out the Playground Personalities – it doesn't matter that you don't know everyone on Spencer's staff. Try and figure out the personality of the team; identify the facts; see where respect came into play; look for the humor and tact. Close the book, and take a moment to analyze the situation. When you open the book, flip back to this page and we can compare notes.

## The Story: Please just do what I ask!

I received a call from Spencer, the president of a professional services firm, asking for a "tune up" meeting. We did a team building meeting several months prior and, although things were good, they were far from perfect. During the original team building exercise, a great deal of trust and respect was built upon and everyone was getting along. When I asked Spencer why a tune up was needed, he told me in his articulate, intelligent, quiet way, "Things are suffering due to the economic crunch. I asked my staff to keep client relations 'on their radar screens' – like make phone calls, finish up projects, offer to have lunch. You know – work."

Apparently, in his mind, staff was ignoring his request and was doing everything but what he had asked them to do. Instead, he thought they were doing other things, thinking that it would please him. Spencer's frustration grew to the point of anger. He could not understand why his staff didn't "just do" what he had asked them to do. It was that simple! As the anger grew, a few minor blow-ups between Spencer and his staff occurred. The staff was confused: Spencer never told them why he was frustrated. Not understanding the situation, they continued to complete more tasks that they thought might make him happy – none of which Spencer asked them to do.

After a few weeks of increasing tension, staff finally approached him and asked, "Why are you not satisfied with the work we are doing?" Spencer replied, "While I am satisfied with the work that is getting done – the work does not make me happy! Doing what I ask makes me happy."

Soon after, I arrived in the conference room to help everyone work through the tension – mixed with a little fear – not a great place to start. As we talked, I felt like the staff was dancing around the issues – and so was Spencer. After an unproductive hour, I called for a break. At the snack machines, I questioned the staff.

"What's going on? Really." I asked. They told me that although they knew Spencer was upset with them, they couldn't figure out what they were doing to make him so mad. When the meeting resumed, I asked Spencer, in front of the entire team, "What would this team have to do in order for you to have your interests met and not be so frustrated with them?"

His reply was priceless and simple: "I just want people to do what I ask them to do. That way, we can stay on top of our client relations until we get through this economic downturn – it's that simple!"

With that said, jaws literally dropped open. The staff was stunned – all of the confusion and hurt feelings could have been avoided if they only followed his directions. The staff began reconnecting with their clients the next morning, tensions lifted and everyone resumed their day-to-day work with a lot less anxiety. Plus, Spencer felt heard, respected and listened to.

### Results: Please just do what I ask!

So, I know you have figured out Spencer's Playground Personality – a classic Steamroller if I ever heard of one! What was the big clue? "If you just do it my way, everything would work out fine." His secondary personality is Peacemaker. Spencer is smart and is able to see the future of his company. He was trying to cut off the inevitable disaster – losing clients – before the economic crisis worsened. As a visionary, he tried to rally the staff to see things the same way he did. His Peacemaker peeked through, instead of coming out "swinging." He tried to be gentle and quiet about his request. Unfortunately, his team missed the ball (and subtle clues). This led to the flare-ups and misunderstandings.

The staff just wanted to make him happy at any cost. Their trying to "get things done" and "make Spencer happy" is classic Organizer and Peacemaker personalities, respectively.

Do you think Spencer had a grasp of his staff's Playground Personalities? I think it is doubtful – he was focused on the things they weren't doing rather than regroup to ask the staff what was going on.

What about respect? Spencer tried to bring the staff together to help out with a potentially difficult situation. His staff responded with a unified front and genuinely tried to support him. That's a good start. The part that concerned me the most was the emotional blow-ups. These were jarring to the staff – and rightly so – to the point where they were worrying about making Spencer happy and not following through with the clients. Not a good situation, and one in which neither could respect the other.

What are the facts? We know that there's an economic downturn, which is a major concern for Spencer. He is critically concerned with keeping client relations at their current levels to prevent their leaving. He wanted them to be called to reassure them of the company's commitment to their relationship. Spencer also knew there was a disconnect between what he asked the staff to do and what his staff was actually doing. He was astute enough to call for help, and knew that it is sometimes best to bring in outside help when you cannot facilitate every issue with your staff.

What about the humor? It's a little difficult to see the absurdity in the story – but it is there. Imagine an upset boss, an overeager staff hoping to please him and random outbursts – not

"Ha ha!" funny, but in retrospect, a nutty situation.

How did Spencer put this all together? Not very well if he resorted to blow-ups. What should Spencer have done differently here? He could have called his staff in to discuss what the economic downturn meant to the business. He could have clearly explained what should be done to secure client relations – and why it's important. He could also have called in each staff member to review the status of their clients and work with them individually to develop strategies to secure the client's business. Because he steamrolled over everyone from the start and did not fully explain the situation to a group of people that needed information up front in order to complete the plan, he never received the staff's buy-in. You can't paddle a canoe without oarsmen.

Whew! That was easy, right? Trust me, it gets easier every day. I could probably dissect this story even more – as could you – but I'm sure you've seen the major points, and how they all affect the situation.

It's easier to see everyone else's mess than to focus in on our own realities. If you were a consultant to Spencer, it would have been easy for you to see the situation. But if you were Spencer, it would have been hard to get that distance to see the field clearly.

When things aren't going the way you want them to go, think of Spencer. Try to stand back from the situation and figure out what you could have done for your team so they could respond to your way of thinking.

# CHAPTER NINE

# Neglected No More

As I wrote on the first page of this book, we all stumble on the next great adventure in life. Sometimes we steer our way towards it, and other times, it is thrust upon us. I wanted to help managers who are promoted and left scratching their heads, discovering that there is a world of difference between being a great employee and managing other employees. This is the wave of the future, as companies look to hire people at their earliest stages of employment who will easily transition into management. In doing so, more people will find themselves saying, *"Oops! I'm the manager!"*

Being "promoted from within" sounds good on paper – one I support with a big caveat. Companies must train people, give them the time to learn and adapt to their new management life, provide a forum for them to come together and give them practical work-life situations to solve – all before they can officially be called a "manager."

However, this commitment is difficult for many organizations – so it's trial by fire. It's because of this lack of training that I wrote this book. Now, it's up to you – the newly-promoted manager – to learn what makes a happy manager, what skills you need to acquire and how you acquire them. Oh yes, and make sure you practice, too!

Most of us recall our school days and a time when we had the chance to take a break from the rigor of class work and go outside to play or hang out. Those days are usually easy to recall and relate to our lives as grown-ups. Remember, being self-aware makes it much easier to recognize the behaviors in others – which is why assessing your own Playground Personality is the first step towards understanding others clearly. You have been reminded of the common sense skills – The Neglected Knowledge: The Forgotten Five – to help you in this endeavor.

So, why did you forget these in the first place? Probably because as a new manager, you were too excited – and overwhelmed – to remember. But now your brain has been jostled to recall what you already know – assess people, be respectful, face facts, find the humor and use tact – are all pretty simple to remember when you lose your way. Don't forget them, and don't neglect them – used wisely, they will lead you to happier and easier times ahead.

*A Nanny Challenge:*

Let's reflect on this final story and put everything you have re-learned to work. Close the book and take a moment to analyze the situation. When you have an answer, come back to the book to confirm your thoughts.

## The Story:  Have a candy dish and a box of tissues

Jack, my friend since childhood, was newly promoted to a supervisor in a prestigious branch of the U.S. Government. He had been fast-tracked throughout his career, and he participated in numerous government-sponsored supervisory skills training programs.

I was at Jack's house on the eve of his first day as a new supervisor. He was excited, confident and ready for his new assignment. We spoke about what he should expect in the coming days, and I suggested that it would be a good idea to get a candy dish, fill it with mints, and put it, as well as a box of tissues, on his desk.

"Why do I need those? Where I work, we have no wimps!" he shot back. The subject was dropped and he changed the topic. On my drive home, I said to myself, "Good going, Kathy." You certainly are famous for giving prematurely unsolicited advice."

A few months went by when I got a call from Jack. He was a little freaked out, to say the least. He explained that one staffer, Pete, came into his office to talk with him. Pete was stressed out due to personal issues at home, as well as a new assignment in the office. As soon as Jack started to inquire about how he could help him, Pete broke down. While requesting some time off to sort out his life, Pete began to weep.

Jack had never experienced a subordinate as upset as Pete. It made Jack uncomfortable, and all he wanted to do was get up and leave. In his mind, he calculated the distance between his chair and the office door, but there was a problem – there was a desk and a broken man between them. Jack had no escape!

At his core, Jack is a compassionate guy – he just never thought he would have to be so at the office. Jack regrouped, focused his attention on Pete, listened to his problems and concerns and offered some consoling advice. As Pete left, Jack thanked him for his openness, and Pete responded with a thank you for being understanding.

That night Jack was caught rummaging through the house. When his wife asked him what he was looking for, he frantically replied, "Some candy and a box of tissues!"

### Results: Have a candy dish and a box of tissues

Jack is highly trained and takes advantage of an opportunity to learn – classic Steamroller. His pooh-poohing of my idea of the candy dish and his remark about "wimps" was also telling.

But here's the turn in the story: instead of running away from the situation, Jack pulled himself up by his bootstraps and spent the time listening to Pete and offering some advice. Jack's got a little Peacemaker in him, also. This makes him a smart and compassionate manager – two critical components for success!

In this story, Pete is probably an Organizer – he needed the time off to "sort" through things. Organizers do a lot of sorting, because it helps them to think more clearly. Pete also was probably physically exhausted trying to manage all he had on his plate. When Organizers reach the point of breaking down – emotionally and physically – it's because they can't keep up with their own lists! They are probably their own worst enemy!

Jack showed Pete a great deal of **respect** by listening and genuinely caring about his issues. In addition, Pete must have a great deal of trust in Jack to have gone to him in the first place with such sensitive and confidential issues.

The **facts** were very basic: Pete was pretty stressed out and needed his boss to listen and give him some direction. In the workplace, issues are usually not always about the work. Managers are often called in to address matters that affect people's work – matters that usually start away from the workplace.

The **funniest** part of this story was Jack trying to escape his own office! Although not too many people walk out of their own offices mid-conference, I think Jack would have liked that option!

And how did Jack use **tact**? A simple and heartfelt "thank you" at the end of the conversation went a long way to sum up the conversation, reinforcing their mutual respect and understanding.

I can't forget about the candy dish and tissues. I was right about this one – and my advice did come back to haunt Jack.

*My final Nanny Tip:* Get a candy dish and tissues. It will be the most appreciated $10 you'll ever spend.

*Extra Credit:*

How would the story have changed if Jack had been an Organizer? Jack might have given Pete the same amount of concern and time, but in the forefront of Jack's mind, he'd have been thinking, "Oh my, who is going to do Pete's work if he goes on leave? How much work does Pete have to do? What has been left undone?" When the conversation ended and Pete left, Jack would have felt pretty stressed, too!

What if Jack had been a Revolutionary? He might have told Pete not to give his work a second thought – the office would pitch in and everyone would get involved to get the work done. The team could absolutely figure it out on their own and make it happen.

*One Last Nanny Challenge*

Can you promise me that you'll think about what you'll do differently at work (and home) now that you have read my book? Consider three things that you can commit to implement, and write them here:

1. _____

2. _____

3. _____

When you find yourself stuck at work or trying to figure out how best to relate to your staff, refer to The Neglected

Knowledge: The Forgotten Five and reflect on your commitments. This will keep you grounded and continuously learning new things about yourself and others.

## A Final Thought

I always say you should take all the unsolicited advice you can throughout your career – it's usually the most compelling. Listen to it when it comes and tuck it away in your mind. You probably won't know you'll need it at the time, but, WOW, it will have an incredible impact when you do use it. And best of all – it's usually free!

As you go through the future as a manager, remember the simple advice of The Corporate Nanny. Refer to me when you get stuck (which you will), and remember that my advice is usually based on common sense. Just ask yourself, "What would The Corporate Nanny do?" It might spur on a whole new solution. But most importantly, remember, I'm not trying to change you – that is a fool's errand. I just want you to realize that you can change. And guess what – you already have.

*The Nanny Cheat Sheet:* **The Peacemaker**

**Peacemakers need to make sure everyone is okay**. They are supportive of and care about others. They are loyal to the company and their staff. Peacemakers do not like conflict. **Identify Peacemakers** by their downward-darting eyes in avoidance of conflict, squirming in their chairs or excusing themselves to the restroom.

**S/he might start a sentence with, "I feel..."**

**Peacemakers show respect by focusing on the person and creating relationships.** You can show respect to them by working collaboratively. They see ignoring or mocking others as disrespect. You can repair their respect, but with diminishing returns.

**Peacemakers collect facts through trusted resources.** They can be given incorrect facts and will not place blame.

**Peacemakers define humor as an element that keeps staff focused.** They use humor with a great deal of respect, looking at the whole situation to bring people together.

**Peacemakers need a detailed plan in time**. They like to manage the big-picture – and often wait for the details. They ask for feedback – and will use it.

## *The Nanny Cheat Sheet:* **The Organizer**

**Organizers manage by scheduling and creating timelines and lists.** They live in a highly structured world and have a high sense of tradition. They are extremely reliable and dependable. **Identify Organizers** by their immediate need to create a schedule or chart!

**S/he might start a sentence with, "I think..."**

**Organizers show respect by valuing hard work.** You can show them respect by quality and quantity of meaningful work with specific deadlines. They see calling in an expert as disrespectful You can never repair an Organizer's respect – so be careful!

**Organizers collect facts through others who had similar experiences.** They ask many questions, and will continue to fact-find until they have closure.

**Organizers define humor as seeing things for what they are.** They use humor to reduce stress and value stepping back to see the humor in a situation to increase team productivity.

**Organizers require detailed plans.** Clear and concise communications are necessary to bring a plan to success. They will invite experts in for a mid-course correction. They manage time well and get impatient with others who do not.

## *The Nanny Cheat Sheet:* **The Revolutionary**

**Revolutionaries hate routine, are action-oriented and like to be in the moment.** They prefer to act now, and beg for forgiveness later. They are outgoing and easy to get along with. **Identify Revolutionaries** by their distraction in conversation (often to have a side conversation) and doodling during meetings.

**S/he might start a sentence with, "I don't like..."**

**Revolutionaries show respect by focusing on the situation and people to bring about a positive solution**. You can show them respect by working on the impossible and doing it with passion. Not taking responsibility for your work is very disrespectful. Their respect can be repaired.

**Revolutionaries collect facts like a professional investigator.** They will ask everyone and anyone for information without a filter to screen out information.

**Revolutionaries define humor as a state of being.** They use humor to get through life's toughest parts. It keeps them grounded.

**Revolutionaries do not like detailed plans**. They would rather "wing it" with a basic structure based on fact. They include everyone in the process and will make mid-course corrections with ease. They quickly join new opportunites, often at the expense of others' sanity.

*The Nanny Cheat Sheet:* **The Steamroller**

**Steamrollers value education, intellect and competence.** They believe they are subject matter experts, and can be perceived as arrogant. **Identify Steamrollers** by credentials, opinions and their straightforward demeanor.

**S/he might start a sentence with, "I believe..."**

**Steamrollers show respect by calling in the experts.** You can show them respect by giving them a difficult assignment and asking for their opinion. Stealing ideas is very disrespectful. Their respect can be earned back if lost.

**Steamrollers collect facts as though they were solving a complex puzzle.** They go to the information source, preferring those with credentials and education.

**Steamrollers define humor in terms of personal reputations.** They use humor to suspend tense moments and will look back at a situation to put things in perspective.

**Steamrollers believe details are not as important as the vision of a plan.** They talk through the big picture and offer up details to the folks who may need some help thinking differently in the future. They make midcourse corrections by communicating to gain trust.

# Epilogue

Throughout my career, I have met too many good people and good employees who get promoted, but can't bask in the glory of their promotion because they are scared to death of the people on the other side of their door! I have always imagined how helpful it would be if people had the inside scoop on how to manage their organizations, departments – and themselves!

That's why I was inspired to write this book. I wanted to make it different from other books. Many times, we read books or go to a training class, but never have the chance to practice what we've learned before we have to act. *Oops! I'm The Manager!* provides a personal opportunity for you to practice as you read along. Our test readers all wished they could have read this book before they were asked to take on their new roles as managers.

I hope you enjoyed reading my book – I had fun writing it! Rest assured, there is more coming. While I'm working on other books and articles, keep up with The Corporate Nanny online at www.thecorporatenanny.net.

Happy managing!